ENDORSEMENTS

I just read through Sally Hanan's *Fix Yourself* workbook and I am so glad that I did. What an awesome toolset for personal development, and also for use to disciple and take others through subjects such as building identity, overcoming lies, God as a Father, and more. One of the things Christians desperately need is tools that help build our inner man, and this is an amazing workbook that will be great for groups, individuals, and married people. Sally has put together prayers, reflections, and work assignments that chart out inner change and help you to see God in the light of his love for you—so that you can fully embrace the true life of healthy self love, love for others, and love for our marvelous God. Bravo for this great book!

— Shawn Bolz
Senior Pastor of Expression58
Author of *The Throne Room Company* & *Keys to Heaven's Economy*

The author of the book of Hebrews reminds us that in order to finish our race, we must "fix our eyes on Jesus, the author and perfecter of our faith." Sally Hanan shows us that part of fixing our eyes on Jesus is fixing ourselves *in* Jesus. The English definition of the word *fix* is to repair or mend; it also means to make fast, firm, or stable. When you become firm and stable in Christ, you become repaired and mended through Christ. This workbook is a wonderful reminder of all that Christ purchased for us on the cross and is a valuable tool to appropriate in our everyday life. *Fix Yourself* is a practical guide to supernatural development that will introduce the reader to all that life can be in Jesus.

— Bob Hazlett
Director of Touch of Fire Ministries
Author of *The Roar: God's Sound in a Raging World*

A well-known speaker came through our city recently. When posed with the question asking where it seemed the favor was evident in ministries in our day, the response was this: "It is apparent that the ministries that God is blessing are those who will put swords in the hands of champions." This speaks strongly, and I wholeheartedly agree, that ministries that empower have found a key component in God's value system. Sally

Hanan is an empowering writer, teacher, instructor, and revivalist. As a key leader in our community, her words have helped to shape the culture of revival for many people, and her willingness to give valuable time in loving people into life has produced numerous testimonies of freedom that replaced years of pain and bondage. I have no doubt that Sally's writings will extend her voice to bring the same freedom to many people all over the world.

— Bill Vanderbush
Director of the Texas School of Supernatural Ministry

This workbook is such a powerful tool in helping one overcome lies and walls that we've built in our hearts and minds regarding God our Father. Everyone has a past, and depending on our experiences, many of us carry out mistrusts, establish vows that are impossible to keep, and repeat failures in life due to relational dysfunctions and past experiences. Sally loads this manual with truth and biblical perspective that will help everyone overcome ungodly beliefs and lies they've believed about themselves or about God. The testimonies of victories that start off each chapter will shed light on areas of weakness you may have had and will cause you to overcome similar mindsets from experiences in your own life. We were very blessed and enriched by reading this book and we know you will be too. We highly recommend this workbook to anyone wanting to walk in freedom and live out a victorious Christian life!

— Jerame & Miranda Nelson
Directors of Living at His Feet Ministries
Author of *Activating Your Spiritual Senses,*
Activating God's Justice, & *Activating Your Dream Language*

—SALLY HANAN—

FIX YOURSELF
IN JESUS

FIRE DRINKERS
PUBLISHING

FIX YOURSELF
IN JESUS

Editing team: Inksnatcher & Superior Editing Services
Cover design team: Inksnatcher & AM Design

First Edition, 2014
ISBN: 978-0991335008
Publisher: Fire Drinkers Publishing

I DEDICATE THIS WORKBOOK TO MY SAINT OF A HUSBAND AND MY TWO GROWN CHILDREN. WITHOUT THEM, I NEVER WOULD HAVE HAD THE SUPPORT AND TIME NEEDED TO DEVELOP THIS GIFT OF HELPING PEOPLE GET CLOSER TO JESUS.

CONTENTS

FOREWORD

ABOUT THE AUTHOR

FOREWORD

I wrote this workbook in order to reach an audience that might not normally have access to an inner healing counselor or mentor. The information inside is based on my time spent with people wanting to let go of the past and move closer to God. What I've discovered is that time spent with him, talking about what's going on, and waiting for his response is by far the best method of inner healing available. While it's difficult sometimes to work through this kind of stuff alone, at least it may become your springboard into the "more" God has for you.

This is in workbook form so that it can be adapted for use in small groups, with a mentor, or in workshops. Each chapter begins with a testimony and then moves into some personal insights about the topic, followed by time for reflection, Scriptures, and a prayer. You can work through the book in the order it's presented, or do a "chapter roulette." I've organized it based on the order of steps people are usually able to handle. You might do one chapter and then leave it for a season; that's absolutely fine too. God is supremely gentle, and everything has its time for action.

Be blessed.

—Sally

MY RELATIONSHIP WITH THE FATHER

Throughout my childhood I was subjected to three fathers, abusive parenting, divorce, abandonment, neglect, alcoholism, the foster care system, and adoption. I was introduced to the best Father of all—God—when I spent weekends with my birth father. We went to church as a family and I learned about God, but I only learned about him; I never got to know him personally. That time with my dad only lasted eighteen months, because my mom decided to give me up for adoption at the age of nine.

I spent the next few decades getting in touch with family members, only to then shut them out again because I had too many expectations of how they should treat me, and I always ended up feeling abandoned or neglected again.

I became an alcoholic, and over time my life fell apart. People kept letting me down, abusing me, using me. I had a miscarriage. Then my adoptive mother got sick—a woman who had the strongest faith I'd ever seen—and during the time I spent with her, I came to realize that if she could get through on faith alone, there was no reason for me to not do the same thing. The night she died was the night I had my last drink. It was as if God was grabbing onto my shoulders, letting me know that I was not going this way anymore. I'd kept doing the same thing with the same results. I was done running the show.

I joined a church and gradually came to experience that not everyone was out to betray me or let me down. I started to have more faith in others, faith in a different kind of people—people God had done things for who then paid it forward by doing things for others. I started to hear the voice of God. Finally I knew I was going to be okay; I knew he had me. I was his. Rather than me offering myself up to him, he took me. I've never looked back.

I started leaning less on other people and more on God to make me okay inside. In AA literature there's a line about trusting God, about how God won't let us down. My heavenly Daddy has the means to care for me that my earthly daddy doesn't. I wouldn't be here if God didn't love me. I was raised by my powerful Father—I don't have to worry about anything, I just do my best. He's got me, and he always has.

—Rita

In many ways, I have transferred my perspective of my father into my view of God. Experience with the visible will do that. Everything we learned as children about how a father acts comes from the foundation of love and acceptance our fathers gave us, so it is no wonder that we can confuse what we saw or never had with what we're told about God's character. It's hard to settle on truth when the past we've experienced firsthand seems so much more real than the words in a book; it's easier to believe that while others may get to have a father/child relationship with God, it's not for us. Besides, is it even something we want?

Life and truth and lies can get muddled up. Lies are birthed in painful experiences, and if your dad was physically, psychologically, or verbally abusive; or if he abandoned you or neglected you, then you more than likely believe your negative thoughts about God to be the truth.

But Jesus, the one closest to his Father, the one who saw God as he was and is and always will be, said otherwise. It's a no-brainer that the one called the Truth is the only one who tells you the truth, so if you think that God doesn't love you or want to live in you or be close to you, it's just not true.

The truth is that God is not like your earthly father.

Even if your father was the best father you could ever imagine having, no one compares to how good and loving God the Father is. He is kind and thoughtful, he is gentle and patient, he is always with us, he is compassionate and gracious, he is slow to anger and quick to love.

Right before Jesus went to the cross, he prayed the prayer that defined his life purpose—that we would be one with the Father, having the same intimacy and love and life in him as Jesus, himself, had. Since his life was sacrificed to bring us into that place of love, we should take another look at the obstacles on the path to our Father's arms.

> In the story of the prodigal son, a man had two sons, both of whom he loved dearly. He shared all he had with both of them, he gave them both total freedom to make their own choices, and he celebrated when they chose to be with him. He didn't yell at the son who ran off and refused to talk to him again, and he didn't get mad at the older son for having a massive pity party when the younger son's return was celebrated. He understood both perspectives and responded in love.

In the same way, God responds in understanding and love to all your questions and doubts and pain, but he wants to be your perfect Father; he wants you to be able to receive his flawless love down in the core of your being, because he knows that only then will you be whole and fully alive in him.

God wants to help you push past the lies about him and hear and receive the truth.

REFLECTION

Take some time and check off everything you think is true about God, even if it sounds untrue in your head. If it feels true in your heart then it's still difficult for you to believe God's truth, because you still hurt inside.

God does not love me.	God does not like me.	God does not protect me.	God does not care about me.
God lets bad things happen to teach me lessons.	God doesn't want me because I am too sinful.	God just puts up with me.	God never wants to talk with me.
God abandons me.	God hates me.	God is mad at me.	God is scary.
God does not understand me.	God enjoys seeing me in pain.	God does not enjoy my company.	God always lets me down.

FINISH THE FOLLOWING SENTENCES

I am angry, frustrated, hurt, or disappointed with God because …

he let

he didn't

he doesn't

he should have

In order for a relationship to be rich in love and friendship, both parties have to be real with each other. This means that God wants you to be real with him, so on page 5 is a guide to help you so that you can let him know what's really going on inside at the heart level.

TRUTH

What is the truth about God, our Father? Mull over the following Scriptures and write down anything that God might be showing you through them.

"So we have come to know and to believe the love that God has for us. God is love, and whoever abides in love abides in God, and God abides in him" (1 John 3:1).

"See what kind of love the Father has given to us, that we should be called children of God; and so we are" (1 John 4:16).

"It is the LORD your God who goes with you. He will not leave you or forsake you" (Deut. 31:6).

"Blessed be the [...] Father of mercies and God of all comfort, who comforts us in all our affliction" (2 Cor. 1:3).

4

"I have called you friends" (John 15:15).

"He is my steadfast love and my fortress, my stronghold and my deliverer, my shield and he in whom I take refuge" (Ps. 144:2).

"For you, O Lord, are good and forgiving, abounding in steadfast love to all who call upon you" (Ps. 86:5).

"You have seen my affliction; you have known the distress of my soul" (Ps. 31:7).

PERSONAL PRAYER (preferably out loud; I find it more effective when speaking openly with God)

God, I am angry/frustrated/hurt/disappointed with you because …

you let

you didn't

you don't

you should have

This is what I have believed to be true about you: (Read off the checked statements from your reflections list.) *I am sorry for judging you to be like my birth father.*

Wait and listen for God's response through your thoughts, feelings, and senses. Write or draw any positive thoughts, mental pictures, feelings, or words God gives you.

NOTES

6

NOTES

7

2
MY INNER VOWS

One night I had a dream that a big black moth was in my childhood home, and it flew across the room right into my mouth. The dream was very vivid, and I could feel the moth's hard little body trying to crawl and wiggle through my lips, which I had clenched shut in the nick of time. I reached up, struggling to grab hold of it and wrench it out of my mouth. I felt it crunch between my fingers and I threw it to the ground, but it was immediately repaired and continued to fly around the room, making repeated attacks against me. Standing behind me was my mother, calmly watching and silently encouraging me to follow the moth around the house.

At first I had no idea what this dream meant, but it felt like a warning of some kind from God. I pondered it for a couple of weeks. Then one day I was talking to my best friend, and she was trying to explain to me that it is necessary to follow your heart at times. With great vehemence I replied with this phrase: "I will never let some man make a fool out of me!"

Immediately the Holy Spirit fell on me, and I was taken back into a memory of my childhood, one that I had forgotten. It was of my mother, telling me over and over again, "Don't you ever let a man make a fool out of you; don't you ever be stupid like Mommy." And over and over again, every time she said this to me, from as early as I can remember, I would vow, "Don't worry, Mommy, I will never do that."

I came out of the flood of memories and heard God say, "You have been enslaved by that vow ever since. That is what the moth is." At this point I fell to the ground under the power of God and proceeded to renounce the vow I had made and give that part of myself back to God. I physically felt a weight and a presence leave me. Since that moment, my thinking and my behavior have been freed. I am able to interact with men freely, without fear and without hindrance. —Rose

Considering that the Bible gives Jacob's story ten chapters, independence (being a lone ranger) must bother God a bit. Jacob started out in life helping himself to the best. He did the daily work of tending the sheep rather than going out and hunting. His deceit in stealing Esau's birthright is a prime example of the way he used whatever he could to get his way. But he learned the hard way that no matter how many self-serving decisions he could make, they were never enough; they never satisfied. It isn't until his fight with the angel of the Lord that we see his change of heart. He didn't want to quit until he knew that God would bless him—he started to look to God instead of his own abilities—and life got richer (Gen. 12-50).

I have no idea when it started, but considering that my first word was *no*, it's no surprise that I didn't trust anyone but myself growing up. I don't even know why—I guess I just had this pervasive feeling that if anything was going to be done on my behalf, I had to be the one to do it. The longer I stayed in school and then boarding school, the more convinced I became that life was more about *me* than the blurry idea of close-knit friends and a prince charming who could love me through any dysfunctional outburst. By the time I was seventeen, I fully believed that I didn't need anyone, and that life would always be that way.

In the young, fragile years of life we see things in a different light, and we interpret events through how they make us feel. Many of us can remember moments when we felt completely alone—in our cribs, in our bedrooms, or at school. Some of us were neglected; other children or people were more important, or we just weren't loved enough, or we didn't matter to those who were supposed to love and cherish us.

We decided that in order to stop feeling the pain of abandonment, we'd protect our little hearts the best way we knew how—we'd put up some walls, and they would be so high and so thick that no one could ever leave us feeling that hurt again. We made vows to ourselves: *I am the only person I will ever trust. I am the only person I will ever rely on. I will never let anyone else make decisions for me.* The problem with walls is that they shut out everyone, good and bad, and they leave us feeling even more alone. *Inner vows shut God out.*

When we shut God out, we shut ourselves off from the only good and perfect Person we can ever have in our lives. If we say we can't hear him or he must talk to everyone else but us, then it's possible that we are the ones who made the wall between us and him so high that he got the message very clearly. God promises that we can be fully alive in him, which means that there is no need for self-protective walls when we're with him.

We make other inner vows, too. We say we will never kiss, never date, never steal, never lie—the list is endless. What we are really saying is that we think we are strong enough to be perfect without Jesus's sacrifice. We may as well forget Jesus and follow some other religion, if that's the case.

Jesus came to be our rock and our strength. We need to let him be exactly that.

REFLECTION

Think back to the first time you felt completely alone. It might even be as far back as the womb. Feel yourself there; don't just watch yourself from afar. Ask Jesus where he was in that place (because he has always been with you), and what he would like to show you about that time. Write down what you see, hear, or feel.

REFLECTION

If you look back at every decision you have made in your life, would you say that each one has been perfect? If you were to line up each decision beside the decisions God could have helped you with, how would they compare? If you are a lone ranger, how does it feel to be the ruler of your world—living by your decisions versus giving God that place?

REFLECTION

In order to get a better picture of exactly how much permission God has to work with you, draw a picture of you on one side of your wall (of permission) and God on the other. Detail the specifications of the wall—how high, how wide, how thick, how long is it?

How did the wall get there?

What might happen to you if the wall were to come down?

Ask God what he wants to do with the wall. Reflect on his answer. If you are too fearful of doing what God says, ask him to give you a tool to help you while you wait on your side of the wall and think about it some more. If you are willing to let him do what he wants, watch as he does it.

TRUTH

What is the truth about God's trustworthiness and presence? Mull over the following Scriptures and write down anything that God might be showing you through them.

"Yet a little while and the world will see me no more, but you will see me. Because I live, you also will live. In that day you will know that I am in my Father, and you in me, and I in you" (John 14:19-20).

"I am not alone" (John 16:32).

"He trusted in the Lord, the God of Israel, so that there was none like him among all the kings of Judah after him, nor among those who were before him" (2 Kings 18:5).

"Some trust in chariots and some in horses, but we trust in the name of the Lord our God" (Ps. 20:7).

"The Lord is my strength and my shield; in him my heart trusts, and I am helped; my heart exults, and with my song I give thanks to him" (Ps. 28:7).

"Trust in him at all times, O people; pour out your heart before him; God is a refuge for us. Selah" (Ps. 62:8).

"Peace I leave with you; my peace I give to you. Not as the world gives do I give to you. Let not your hearts be troubled, neither let them be afraid" (John 14:27).

PERSONAL PRAYER

Father, I'm sorry for relying on my own strength and willpower, and for making vows based on my own abilities instead of yours. I'll receive every bit of the Holy Spirit's help from now on. I want to be more and more like you every day. From now on, the strength I need will come from you instead of my to-do list. My growth is yours to empower, and I'll rest in your ability instead of my own.

If there are any other walls around my heart that need to come down, please show me what they are and help me to willingly let you remove them.

Wait and listen for God's response through your thoughts, feelings, and senses. Write or draw any positive thoughts, mental pictures, feelings, or words God gives you.

NOTES

14

NOTES

15

3

JUDGING MYSELF

I was the master of introspection for most of my teenage years and well into my twenties. I was the one who was too loud or too quiet, too annoying, too attention-seeking, too needy, too lazy, too stupid, too selfish, too cheap. The list was endless. It wasn't until I went through the loss of everything I held dear that I was willing to face myself head on, and start taking a realistic look at what I saw. And what I saw surprised me. While I had spent years watching and critiquing myself, trying to turn myself into a better person by imitating others, I saw instead a woman who had wasted years by never fully living. She had split herself into two parts—one who watched and criticized, and one who tried to measure up and never could.

It took a few more years before I finally managed to accept myself completely and stop making myself a daily to-do list of how I could be better. My critic started to keep quiet, focus on the positive, and move back into the person she was designed to be, and I began to live life as a whole person instead of as an insufferable child and her never-satisfied judge.

—Kristie

Rest in being you. Striving to be like someone else is really
tiring and will only ever get you into second-best place.

All of us have a moment of conception. Of the millions in the race, one sperm managed to push its way past the egg's outer wall and break into its home for the next nine months. That mix of egg and sperm is you or me.

Many of us feel that we were not wanted, or that we were the wrong gender, or that we were accidents. The thing is, though, that at your moment of conception God had a choice. Would he breathe his life into that embryo or would he let it die? He chose to give you life. So why did he do it? Did he not know what you would become? Did he not know what you would be like?

God knew exactly who you would be, and he wanted you here for a reason.

> Jesus was obviously a wanted child. Like a proud father, God never shut up about him in the Old Testament. Neither did the prophets, and don't even mention the brouhaha in the first eighteen months of Jesus's life—between the shepherds and wise men and angels lighting up the sky....

That's all fine, you might say, but you have so many faults and things you hate about yourself that you don't know where to begin. But God created you, and as your creator he is the only one who has the right to name you. Have you let other people name you as fat, short, ugly, selfish, dim-witted, lazy, no good? These can be called lies you believe by osmosis—you have heard them so often from someone who claims to love you that you have come to believe them.

The only person to stop you from moving forward is you. If you were to change your perspective and look at yourself the way a best friend would, would you tell yourself the same things? God needs you here, and he loves how unique you are; he loves the perfect mix of skills and personality traits he gave you. If he is the God of truth, then seeing yourself any differently than he does is seeing yourself through a lying filter.

God is the only one who has the right to be our judge because he is the only one who can see everything that goes on from a heavenly perspective. If you see yourself as anything other than his perfect creation, then what you've done is taken God's job from him as judge. It was not yours to take.

God adopts us into his family for a reason—because he loves us as much as he loves Jesus. We were designed to be with him forever, and he's delighted to call us his own. In my mind, the party in heaven when we were born was just as big as it was for Jesus, and that was before we had even done anything for him! And now he still loves us the same way, even after all our messy attempts at life.

True discernment sees the distant light in someone's future rather
than the shadowed darkness of his past. ~ Lisa Bevere

You are not your past. You are one of God's gifts to the world, and you are the only one designed as you are, which makes you an incredibly unique gift. Downsizing who you are will not bring glory to God. Living in line with your design (his unique blueprint for you) will glorify him.

REFLECTION
Make a list of all the things you don't like about yourself.

Picture yourself giving that list to God and watch him to see what he does with it. Write down what you see him do.

REFLECTION
Look at yourself through God's eyes and write down what he sees.
Are you surprised?

REFLECTION
"When we have our thinking governed by grace and mercy and truth, it sets us free to establish our real identity. When you think that you are a sinner, it means you will doubt the glory and the freedom that belongs to you in Jesus. A sinner mindset cannot generate new life. Any mindset focused on a negative makes us captives to the enemy" ~ Graham Cooke. Do you see yourself as the saint you are? Write down your thoughts.

TRUTH

What is the truth about you? Mull over the following Scriptures and write down anything that God might be showing you through them.

"Is not he your father, who created you, who made you and established you?" (Deut. 32:6).

"For we are God's masterpiece. He has created us anew in Christ Jesus, so we can do the good things he planned for us long ago" (Eph. 2:10).

JUDGING
MYSELF

"'In him we live and move and have our being' as even some of your own poets have said, 'For we are indeed his offspring'" (Acts 17:28).

20

"I praise you because I am fearfully and wonderfully made; your works are wonderful, I know that full well" (Ps. 139:14).

"The partner of a thief hates his own life" (Prov. 29:24).

"Even the hairs of your head are all numbered. Fear not; you are of more value than many sparrows" (Luke 12:7).

PERSONAL PRAYER

Father, I am sorry for taking your job from you. You are the only judge who is fair and full of justice and mercy. The way you see me is the truth. I promise that from now on I will only look at myself through your eyes and act accordingly. Here's your job back.

I am sorry for hating and rejecting myself—someone you put so much love and thought into. Thank you for making me unique, and that just by being myself I can help others in significant ways. Thank you for making me your gift to humanity at this time in history.

Wait and listen for God's response through your thoughts, feelings, and senses. Write or draw any positive thoughts, mental pictures, feelings, or words God gives you.

NOTES

22

NOTES

4 FORGIVING MYSELF

I was leading a double life when I was a senior in high school. I was a leader in my youth group and a nanny for two children. I made all As in school, was a "big sister" mentor, and had a pretty good relationship with my parents—but I was also having sex with my boyfriend. There was a lot of sneaking around, justifying, and lying. For a while I would ask God to forgive me, but then I stopped doing that because I knew I was just going to do it again. After a few months of this behavior, I found out I was pregnant. Now everyone would know my double life because I couldn't hide it anymore. I couldn't seem perfect and yet be pregnant as a senior in high school, so Sam and I looked into an abortion. I went in for the appointment early one morning after having told a very intricate lie to my parents, but as soon as I saw the ultrasound, I knew I couldn't go through with it. At twelve weeks the fetus actually looked like a baby, and the full force of what I was doing hit me like a brick. I went out to the waiting room and Sam was asleep on the couch. He didn't seem to care one way or another, so I decided that this was not the right choice to make. After a very tumultuous pregnancy full of shame, guilt, and self-condemnation, I had a healthy baby boy.

I stayed ashamed of how Caleb came about because I couldn't move on and forgive myself. When people I didn't know would comment on how cute he was, I would make it a point to lie and talk about "my husband." Even after Sam and I were married, I would lie about how long we had been married. As Caleb grew up, he started showing signs of the shame that I was putting on him—he was extremely shy, hid things, and started to stutter. I was still so embarrassed. I knew that God forgave me, but never realized that all of my odd behavior stemmed from not forgiving myself.

I finally heard a message at church that shook that shame loose. I remember breaking down with a friend who prayed for me. Then she led me in a short but powerful prayer to forgive myself and break the power of shame. Caleb didn't deserve shame. He did nothing to deserve condemnation, and yet I couldn't see past my own mistake to remove that shame. Everything changed when I was able to confidently own the mistake but look at it through Jesus's eyes. I saw my beloved boy as a child of God and a gift that God had given me. I saw myself as a redeemed woman with a powerful testimony and a bright future. I was able to more fully love myself and my family, and more importantly, fully accept the love and forgiveness of God. Once I told Caleb that I was proud and grateful he was my son, the stuttering and nervousness went away almost immediately. You can't fully accept the love of God if you hold unforgiveness toward anyone, including yourself.

—Britt

When I look at the things I regret in life, most of them include the hurting of other people. Either I said words I shouldn't have said, or I didn't follow through with something I promised, or I helped myself to something that wasn't mine to take. Perhaps the hardest memories to get over are the ones that involved my kids—why wasn't I there, why did I do that, why didn't I do that for them? We have all done things we are ashamed of—the could-haves, the should-haves, the if-onlys. If only I hadn't gone to that party … if only I had told my mom I loved her; if only….

> I'm sure Peter was horrified to watch himself hurt Jesus, literally word by word, in that courtyard. "No, I don't know him. I don't know the one man who has changed my life and heart and soul. I don't know the man who has poured his life into mine for the last three years." There is a lot of material there that could have tortured him for years—words and should-haves and could-haves that could have forced him to hide out at home for the rest of Jesus's time on earth, in order to wallow in his weakness and fear. Interestingly, Peter's next encounter with Jesus gave him the opportunity to affirm his love for Jesus and to accept the call on his life. *Peter's disastrous words didn't change how Jesus saw him.* (Read John 18 & 21.)

Jesus knows every single thing we have done, and he knows our regrets. We have often heard that it's good to keep on reminding ourselves of our sinful past because it keeps us in our place; it keeps us humble. This is another lie. Shame is from Satan, because shame leads us into deeper and deeper despair. Godly sorrow leads to repentance and hope. *Godly sorrow leads us to God and freedom. Guilt leads us to our own efforts and slavery.*

Godly sorrow is when we see our sin the way God does, when we see we have sinned against him and we see his heart for us and those around us. "Against thee, thee only have I sinned" (Ps. 2:4). Godly sorrow brings us back into the place where his will is our will and his heart is our heart—the goal of our salvation. Self-forgiveness frees us up to focus on God's goodness and guidance instead of our failures, and we become free to see our place in life from God's perspective again.

> *"I think that if God forgives us we must forgive ourselves. Otherwise, it is almost like setting up ourselves as a higher tribunal than Him."* ~ C.S. Lewis

Jesus died on the cross so we could be completely free from all sin and shame and guilt. He died with every single sin we have ever committed, along with every single sin we will commit in the future. All we need to do is acknowledge the godly sorrow we feel for our sin and receive his forgiveness yesterday, today, and forever.

> *You are no longer a sinner. You have been saved by grace and are now a saint, a child of God adopted into his family and alive in the Spirit.*

If you look at all your regrets as if they are dirty laundry, all you have is a load that keeps turning in the drum. There's no detergent in there, no rinse and spin, just a dry load in the washing machine waiting for a cleansing. Each spin calls out your name, telling you that your sin defines you; your sin is who you really are; you'll never be clean enough. When you need something to wear, you pull something out of the dirty drum. Rather than walk around with dirty laundry on your back, are you willing to let your laundry go through the full wash and then dry it and walk around in fresh clothing?

REFLECTION
Write about the reasons why you'd rather not forgive yourself.

REFLECTION
Talk to Jesus about your difficulty in letting go of your shame.

REFLECTION
Talk to Jesus about the effects your shame has on the way you live life and on those around you.

REFLECTION
Write down his response.

TRUTH

What is the truth about self-forgiveness? Mull over the following Scriptures and write down anything God shows you through them.

"Against thee, thee only have I sinned" (Ps. 2:4).

"For godly grief produces a repentance that leads to salvation without regret, whereas worldly grief produces death" (2 Cor. 7-10).

"The law of the Spirit of life has set you free in Christ Jesus from the law of sin and death.... If Christ is in you, although the body is dead because of sin, the Spirit is life because of righteousness. If the Spirit of him who raised Jesus from the dead dwells in you, he who raised Christ Jesus from the dead will also give life to your mortal bodies through his Spirit who dwells in you" (Rom. 8:1-2, 10-11).

28

"For to set the mind on the flesh is death, but to set the mind on the Spirit is life and peace. For the mind that is set on the flesh is hostile to God" (Rom. 8:6).

"How much more will the blood of Christ, who through the eternal Spirit offered himself without blemish to God, *purify our conscience from dead works* to serve the living God" (Heb. 9:14; emphasis mine).

"Let us draw near with a true heart in full assurance of faith, with our hearts sprinkled clean from an evil conscience" (Heb. 10:22).

PERSONAL PRAYER

Father, I'm sorry for the things I have done that did not glorify you or show love to myself—and I'm specifically sorry for:

_____

_____

_____

(Name them internally or share them out loud while praying this prayer.)

You died on the cross for every single sin I have ever committed. I give you all the should-haves, could-haves, and if-onlys, and I receive your forgiveness for them. Your blood is enough. I am clean. I am free.

I also make the choice today to forgive myself. I choose to see myself the way you do. I choose to release myself from all judgments the way you do. Your blood is enough. I am clean. I am free.

Thank you, Lord, that you don't condemn me anymore because you removed all my sin on the cross. Thank you that every single thing I have ever done or will do has been paid for and I no longer have any part in death. I step into your life, your light, and your truth. I set my mind on the things of the Spirit, who gives me life and peace. I choose to live in the Spirit. He is life.

I am no longer a sinner who occasionally gets to be righteous. I am a saint who occasionally stumbles. I am my Father's holy child.

Wait and listen for God's response through your thoughts, feelings, and senses. Write or draw any positive thoughts, mental pictures, feelings, or words God gives you.

NOTES

30

NOTES

JUVENILE
PROBATE
COURTROOM
JUDGE
R.H. HOOVER

COURTROOM
NO. 1

JUDGING OTHER PEOPLE 5

My family had just moved to Canada. My oldest son had started pre-K, and I thought it would be a good time to meet others and make friends. Over the next week, whenever I met a mom, I'd mentally go through my list to see if she'd be a likely or unlikely future friend. One day, a woman came in with two boys. She had obviously just worked out, so she made it onto my "no" list. After about four weeks of my avoiding her and talking to all the other moms, she walked up to me and asked if she had done anything to offend me.

I was stunned, said no (because I would look stupid if I admitted that her working out had put her on my "no" list), and she invited me for lunch. At her house she broke into tears and told me her life story, and said she needed someone to pray with her and help her to find her way back to Jesus. She told me that the first time she saw me, she felt that I would be the person she would talk to, and she couldn't believe that I was avoiding her. That was a lesson for me!

—Ruth

God has made each person for a unique reason, and generations of individuals are here right now because they have purposes to fulfill. In the same way that we have no right to judge ourselves, neither do we have the right to judge others. "And to God, the judge of all …" (Heb. 3:23). Satan is called many names in the Bible: slanderer, adversary, worthless, filthiness, wickedness, craftiness, evil power, tempter, accuser, evil one, god of this age, prince of demons, and the ruler of the kingdom of the air. He is the real source of all evil and pain, and our anger should be directed at him.

When we judge others, even those we feel justified in judging, we partner with Satan; we work with him at his level. We become the accusers, the slanderers, the adversaries. We base our judgments on appearances, hearsay, offences, and assumptions. All our judgments pile up into a thick wall that prevents us from reaching hearts with the character and love of Jesus. (We'll talk more about those who have deeply wounded us in the next chapter.)

Sometimes the air is so thick with your judgments that their clouds obstruct your vision. We may frequently justify our judgments with facts, but in reality, facts are only part of the equation. Justice is about the whole story, and God is the only one who has the right to judge others because he is the only one who can see everything that goes on from a heavenly perspective. He is the only one who can judge their hearts.

> When Samuel went to find the next king of Israel, he was very taken with Jesse's sons. He seemed to think that Eliab was "the one" based on his height and appearance, but God said that he was not. Even Samuel could have been fooled into anointing the wrong son if he had not known God's voice, and God was clearly telling him that the son with the heart of a king was not in the lineup. God sees everything that matters. (Read 1 Sam. 16.)

A judge is the authority, the one who arbitrates, the expert, the referee. They are the ones who fully assess the actions and consequences of a crime and then make a decision based on those details. They are the ones who decide on the punishment. Healthy judgment is the kind that sees what's going on in a person and sits with that person to listen, to care, to encourage, to support (see 1 Thess. 5:14-15). Many times when we become judges, we stir up bitterness and conflict rather than demonstrate God's love. We cause others to see people differently too, because of the labels and stories we spread around. We cut ourselves off from potential friends and positive connections. And consider that perhaps the overwhelming desire to put someone "in his or her place" is because you are unaware of the value and power of your place. *Well that person …, and that woman! Did you hear that she …? Don't even mention that politician's name … and what about that celebrity who …?*

We cannot see the heart, but God can. We never hear the whole story, but God does. We reject and shut people off, but God lets them in.

Let's be more like him.

REFLECTION

Look at family and friends you love through God's eyes and write down what he sees.

REFLECTION

Look at those who have hurt you through God's eyes and write down what he sees.

REFLECTION

Consider what you notice about people when you first meet them. Do you look for their hearts, their unique designs, your commonalities? Do you listen for God's voice? Do you see what God sees? Write down the names of people you have judged based on hearsay or appearance, and ask God to help you see them through his eyes instead.

TRUTH

What is the truth about judgment? Mull over the following Scriptures and write down anything God shows you through them.

"Do not speak evil against one another, brothers. The one who speaks against a brother or judges his brother, speaks evil against the law and judges the law. But if you judge the law, you are not a doer of the law but a judge. There is only one lawgiver and judge, he who is able to save and to destroy. But who are you to judge your neighbor?" (James 4:11-12).

"Do not judge by appearances, but judge with right judgment" (John 7:24).

"For God did not send his Son into the world to condemn the world, but in order that the world might be saved through him" (John 3:17).

"Judge not, that you be not judged. For with the judgment you pronounce you will be judged, and with the measure you use it will be measured to you. Why do you see the speck that is in your brother's eye, but do not notice the log that is in your own eye?" (Matt. 7:1-5).

"For the Lord sees not as man sees: man looks on the outward appearance, but the Lord looks on the heart" (1 Sam. 16:7).

PERSONAL PRAYER

Father, I am sorry for hating and rejecting others—people you put so much love and thought into. Help me to recognize the sin and not hate the person whom the sin came through. Help me to see others through your eyes all the time, and to keep my anger aimed at the devil, who originates all evil.

Father, I am sorry for taking your job from you. You are the only judge who is fair and full of justice and mercy. The way you see others is the truth. I promise that from now on I will only look at others through your eyes and act accordingly. Here's your job back.

Wait and listen for God's response through your thoughts, feelings, and senses. Write or draw any positive thoughts, mental pictures, feelings, or words God gives you.

NOTES

38

NOTES

6

FORGIVING OTHER PEOPLE

I went through a time in my life when my heart was crushed and bleeding. I was abandoned and betrayed by those closest to me, and I didn't know if I would ever recover or feel whole again. It seemed like a natural plan to stay in unforgiveness. By refusing to forgive, I was able to justify everything I had done over the year. I was good; they were bad. My perspective was white; theirs was black. I was the saintly one; they were the sinners who I wanted to see suffer.

I started a notebook; in it I wrote about every terrible thing that had been done to me and said about me. When I felt that my perpetrators were not suffering enough for what they had done, I'd go back and read it again to feed my sense of justice. The problem with feeding on pain and anger, though, is that we become the very thing we eat. My heart was becoming heavier and uglier every time I went back for another helping.

In the end, I decided to shred that notebook. I took each page and watched it go through the shredder, and with each page chopped into little pieces, my heart felt lighter and freer than it had for a long time. A few months later, God had gotten me to the point when I was able to bless those people and wish them well. My unforgiveness and hopes for revenge were never going to change them anyway, and when I released them into God's arms, I knew that he could do a better job of wooing them and helping them live in a way that was truer to their design. Love wins far more battles than hatred and anger.

—Sandie

In the same way that Jesus knows every single thing we have done, he also knows every single thing about the people who have hurt us. We sometimes keep on reminding ourselves of the things that were done to us so that we can keep the hate going. We think that if we treat the people who hurt us with hate and contempt, it will help us to eventually feel better. This is another lie. Hatred and contempt, offences and resentment are from Satan. When we try to manipulate others into repentance, we're operating in exactly the same way Satan would—we're trying to use shame and guilt to make someone do what we want. Our end goal is not to see them in heaven, it's to cater to our own desires for a safe place. At its worst, unforgiveness mentally delegates people to hell.

> Jesus's life demonstrates the exact opposite heart. So many people gave him cause for unforgiveness—Herod tried to kill him when he was little; Judas betrayed him; Peter denied him; Roman soldiers whipped him, mocked him, and pressed piercing thorns into his head; his disciples slept in his worst hours of anguish before he went to the cross; his family said he was crazy. And yet he hung on that cross and asked his Father to forgive everyone. He took all of their evil into his sinless body and died with it so that we wouldn't have to live with it.

Resentment is like taking poison and hoping the other person dies. ~ St. Augustine

Jesus died on the cross so everyone could be completely free from all sin and shame and guilt. He died with every single sin every person has ever committed, along with every single sin we will commit in the future. We've been forgiven completely. Do we deserve forgiveness more than the ones we are not forgiving? What gives us this right? Our sense of justice is usually warped. We act as if our unforgiveness will bring about the justice we seek, when the reality is that it will never change the ones we now call enemies. All it will do is blacken our hearts.

I find it interesting that Jesus says that the Father will not forgive us of our sins unless we forgive the sins of others (read Matt. 6:14-15). I can only imagine why, but my thoughts are that unforgiveness is a two-edged sword. On our side, it hardens our hearts and fills them with all sorts of things that cause us to pull away from the character of God and line up, instead, with the nature of Satan. On the other side is the soul of the one we won't forgive, and our words and thoughts carry such power that they form chains around that person's soul to the point that they may prevent him or her from receiving Christ.

A friend of mine struggled horribly for a long time when it came to forgiving her father, who had done every awful thing to her that one can imagine a man doing. God spoke to her and asked her if she wanted her father in hell, and while she knew that she wanted to see him suffer in many ways, she did not want him in hell for all eternity. That was her turning point. She forgave him from the heart and handed him over to the Father so that God could administer the kind of justice that only God can give.

REFLECTION
Ask yourself: Has your unforgiveness helped others to change in any way?

REFLECTION
List the people whom you have difficulty forgiving.

REFLECTION
Are you willing to release them from your judgments, your opinions, and your desires for revenge? Why or why not?

Through the eyes of Jesus, take a moment to look again at those people who have hurt you. Do you trust Jesus to bring justice if you release them from your idea of justice—your desires to see others hurt as much as they have hurt you? Discuss that with Jesus in the form of a letter to him.

REFLECTION
Those you hold unforgiveness over might end up in hell because of the lock of your judgments on their souls. Is that okay with you?

TRUTH

What is the truth about forgiveness? Mull over the following Scriptures and write down anything God shows you through them.

"Repay no one evil for evil, but give thought to do what is honorable in the sight of all. If possible, so far as it depends on you, live peaceably with all" (Rom. 12:17).

"For if you forgive others their trespasses, your heavenly Father will also forgive you, but if you do not forgive others their trespasses, neither will your Father forgive your trespasses" (Matt. 6:14-15).

"'Please pardon the iniquity of this people, according to the greatness of your steadfast love, just as you have forgiven this people, from Egypt until now.' Then the Lord said, 'I have pardoned, according to your word'" (Num. 14:19-21).

"And whenever you stand praying, forgive, if you have anything against anyone, so that your Father also who is in heaven may forgive you your trespasses" (Mark 11:25).

"For this is my blood of the covenant, which is poured out for many for the forgiveness of sins" (Matt. 26:28).

PERSONAL PRAYER

Father, I'm sorry for judging those people who have hurt me through my own filter of justice instead of through your all-knowing perspective of love and mercy. Only you know their hearts. I give you _____

_____

(name the people) and push them into your arms. Please take care of them and their sin from now on. I trust you to bring justice and mercy, and I give you any hatred and unforgiveness I hold toward them.

I completely forgive _____

_____

(name the people). I choose to release them from all my judgments. I am sorry for vowing to hurt them as much as they have hurt me. Please lead them to you and help them to know your love.

Wait and listen for God's response through your thoughts, feelings, and senses. Write or draw any positive thoughts, mental pictures, feelings, or words God gives you.

NOTES

46

NOTES

7
MY IDENTITY

I'm not the type of person who likes to take risks because I'm afraid of failure. I was the oldest, so I always felt that I couldn't make mistakes. As a grown woman, I felt caged in by my fear. I was going to suffocate if I didn't get out of it. I signed up for a weekly school of supernatural (Holy Spirit) ministry in a nearby town, and I got a prophetic word in one of them—that I had a lot of ideas about things I could do, but I needed to step out and do them or they would never be done. That got me thinking.

I have always felt that I would end up being some sort of speaker, so I signed up for a comedy course to explore how to release that side of myself. One of the challenges of the class was that I had to put together a fifteen-minute set and present it on stage. I fought my fears all the way, praying for boldness and confidence, not wanting to do it, but knowing I had to in order to grab my chance to be free.

I did it, and it was one of the most memorable nights of my life. I really enjoyed myself, and I walked away from that knowing that I do have talent and that taking risks can be an adventure. Doing it also moved me one step forward into making me more comfortable in my identity.

—Yessenia

When I watched our children, it was relatively easy to see their unique designs early on. Our daughter loved to read, to think, to spend time online, to create, and to try new things. These days she works as a tech support guru, transcriptionist, and graphic designer. Our son enjoyed asking questions, watching others from a distance, challenging statements, coming up with inventive ideas, and giving wisdom when it was asked for. I think he'll end up in design engineering and be an on-the-job counselor. Even when I look back at my own life, I can see highlighted moments of joy—moments when I felt whole with life and fullness. There were obvious things I was drawn toward doing, and that's because I was designed to do them.

"I would rather be what God chose to make me than the most glorious creature that I could think of; for to have been thought about, born in God's thought, and then made by God, is the dearest, grandest and most precious thing in all thinking." ~ George MacDonald

> Both Saul and David were perfectly designed for their roles in life. Saul was well built, strong, strategic, decisive, a visionary, accomplished. He was an excellent choice for the king of Israel … if only his character had matched his gifts.
>
> David was humble, athletic, charismatic, relational, brave, passionate. His love of the Lord and his desire to walk in God's ways added much to his legacy, which has lasted through the generations (1 Sam. 9 & 1 Sam. 16).

Just like Saul and David, we are designed to fit perfectly into our roles today. Many of our skills, strengths, and personality traits have been obvious since we were small. Others have been developed over time and through experience, but all of them have been given to us by God, and they are ours to steward.

When we do what we're designed to do, it comes naturally, without effort; we come alive. Our faces almost glow with life. We're designed this way on purpose by God so that we can live a full life in his presence. The truth about you is that you're not just liked and loved by God—you're also awesome by design, and you're here to do so much more than suck air! Jesus did not only die so you could be holy; he died so you could live life just like him—by living out your great design and purpose in full Technicolor.

I once sat with a woman who was unable to stop crying because she wasn't like anyone else, but then God spoke and told her that her differences were the most awesome things about her. God loves our uniqueness, our quirkiness, our laughs, our smiles, the way we run, our dance moves. He loves it all. We need to rest in that.

If we really knew who God created us to be, we would never want to be someone else. ~ Bill Johnson

REFLECTION

God wanted you to be here with your particular set of skills and talents and personality traits. So what is it about you that he wanted to give life to so badly? Take some time to write down some of the things you know to be true about yourself. Only focus on the positive traits.

Skills/talents

Character and personality traits

REFLECTION

Look back at your life through the lens of your design. How have your personality traits, your natural abilities, your interests, your struggles, and your learned skills combined to bring you to the day-to-day life you live today and the life you hope to live tomorrow?

How have all of the above factors affected your choice of ministries?

TRUTH

What is the truth about God's design of you? Mull over the following Scriptures and write down anything God shows you through them.

"For he chose us in him before the creation of the world […] In love he predestined us to be adopted as his sons through Jesus Christ, in accordance with his pleasure and will" (Eph. 1:4-5)

"Grace was given to each one of us according to the measure of Christ's gift. […] And he gave the apostles, the prophets, the evangelists, the shepherds and teachers, to equip the saints for the work of ministry, for building up the body of Christ" (Eph. 4:7,11-12).

"For you formed my inward parts; you knitted me together […] I am fearfully and wonderfully made. Wonderful are your works […] I was being made in secret, intricately woven in the depths of the earth. Your eyes saw my unformed substance; in your book were written, every one of them, the days that were formed for me, when as yet there was none of them" (Ps. 139:13-16).

"For we are his workmanship, created in Christ Jesus for good works, which God prepared beforehand, that we should walk in them" (Eph. 2:10).

"When each part is working properly, [it] makes the body grow so that it builds itself up in love" (Eph. 4:16).

PERSONAL PRAYER

Thank you, Father, that I am perfectly designed to fit in this world. Thank you for giving me my strengths and interests and personality. Thank you that I'm different to everyone around me, and that you've done that on purpose so that I can fill a space that no one else can. I have been given so much, and I choose to give you glory as my creator by enjoying who you've made me to be.

Wait and listen for God's response through your thoughts, feelings, and senses. Write or draw any positive thoughts, mental pictures, feelings, or words God gives you.

NOTES

54

NOTES

55

8
MY SURRENDER

When I was sixteen, I had seen enough of the Spirit-filled life to know that the Holy Spirit was what I wanted and needed, but I also knew that I couldn't ask until I was willing to surrender everything to God. This freaked me out for a whole year — I couldn't bear the thought of having to obey God on every single thing. My biggest fear was that he'd send me to Africa and I'd end up living in a mud hut in the middle of nowhere with armies of ants and indescribable bugs crawling over me every night.

Obviously, I didn't know God very well, and I certainly didn't trust him enough — but at the same time I knew that surrender was a big deal. I was signing up for all or nothing, not just the parts I liked. Was I willing to die for him? Willing to talk to people about him? Willing to look totally stupid for him? I already only had a handful of friends, and if I turned into a radical, all-out Jesus lover, I was afraid that I'd be completely alone.

But my hunger for more of God won over my fears, and at seventeen I knelt by my bed and told him he could have it all — he could pick my friends, my husband, my career, the places I'd live, everything. And go figure, as soon as I handed it all over I felt the peace and warmth and uncontainable presence of God fill every part of me. The Holy Spirit hasn't left me since that day, in spite of other stupid things I've done and said, and his presence is like a bottomless well. Best decision I ever made.

Years and decades later, while God never operates in ways I expect, we are now a team. He is my friend, and each day can become an adventure when I am sensitive to his voice.

—Fran

Surrender, obedience—even the very words can dial up strong emotions. Some of us want to instantly do the exact opposite. We'd rather go running and screaming into the streets in rush hour before ever allowing someone or something else the authority to tell us what to do. But think about that. Surrender and obedience are the natural offshoots of trust, and when we trust the One we love (to walk with us in order to bring love and beauty into this world), running in the other direction makes no sense. We either trust our Father or we don't. He either is or isn't who he says he is, and if he is, then we need to flow with him in every ripple until this river reaches the ocean. No great movement has ever reached its zenith by having its supporters rally from the sidelines. No, its members show up en masse to strategize and plan and move as one in order to achieve their goals. In the same way, God wants to strategize and plan and move as one with us, our hearts intertwined in love so that people can see heaven everywhere.

Obedience is a weapon, not a weakness—the more we become one with Jesus, the more powerful we are. Paul told the Ephesians that our goal is "attaining to the whole measure of the fullness of Christ" (Eph. 4:13). The way to do that is to let as much of him in as possible until every internal obstacle flows away.

Submission is a sign of a love connection, not external pressure. ~ Danny Silk

In their first encounter, Jesus told Peter to drop his nets on the other side of the boat. Even though Peter thought he knew better (because he'd been fishing all night with no results), he did what Jesus said to do and the boat almost capsized with the amount of fish he caught in the net. Working with Jesus is a blessing, not something to be afraid of. When our will is God's will, it means that we have become so much of a couple that we can finish each other's thoughts, just like couples married for years do. Things get done around the house together, two cups of tea are made, everything becomes instinctual. Even when seasons change and hardships come, the two flow as one. There is a level of trust and respect and value in that relationship that has come into fullness, and the combined force of love is a strong and shining light in the center of everything it reaches.

Obedience to God's will keeps us safe. It keeps us in the protection of his loving arms and on the right path to the fulfillment of our purposes and life message. We know his voice so clearly that we follow even the smallest whispers, and grow into him faster than our counterparts who are still lost in the mire of their struggle to trust him completely. Many of us grew up with controlling parents, and that's because they were taught that obedience is gained by controlling through fear. Threats abound, voices are raised, isolation is common. Growing up with controlling parents may have led us to believe that obedience is far from safe—that to obey means pain. God is not like our parents. He is safe and loving and gentle. He knows and protects our hearts.

We say: "Show me and I will trust you."
Papa says: "Trust me and I will show you." ~ Leif Hetlund

REFLECTION

When you hear the words *surrender* and *obedience,* what emotions and thoughts spring up?

— I feel safe.
— I feel loved.
— I feel scared.
— I want to run the other way.
— I feel pressured.
— I feel the burden of expectations on me.
— I love the challenge.
— I'm excited about going deeper into God's heart.

Talk to the Father about this and write down his response.

REFLECTION

In Christ, we have a new identity and a new purpose for living. The new self is to be one with Jesus, who showed us what God is like when living in the flesh. What do you think will happen to you if you surrender your will to his?

Again, talk to the Father about this and write down his response.

TRUTH

What is the truth about surrender? Mull over the following Scriptures and write down anything God shows you right now through them.

"… until we all attain to the unity of the faith and of the knowledge of the Son of God, to mature manhood, to the measure of the stature of the fullness of Christ, so that […] speaking the truth in love, we are to grow up in every way into him who is the head, into Christ, […] to be like God in true righteousness and holiness" (Eph. 4:22-24, 15).

"So if there is any encouragement in Christ, any comfort from love, any participation in the Spirit, any affection and sympathy, complete my joy by being of the same mind, having the same love, being in full accord and of one mind" (Phil. 2:1-3).

MY
SURR-
ENDER

60

"The Lord is my strength and my shield; in him my heart trusts, and I am helped; my heart exults, and with my song I give thanks to him" (Ps. 28:7).

"And we all, with unveiled face, beholding the glory of the Lord, are being transformed into the same image from one degree of glory to another. For this comes from the Lord who is the Spirit" (2 Cor. 3:18).

"Have I not commanded you? Be strong and courageous. Do not be frightened, and do not be dismayed, for the Lord your God is with you wherever you go" (Josh. 1:9).

PERSONAL PRAYER

Father, I forgive my parents for teaching me that obedience is not safe. I break all internal attachments to the fear of obedience to your perfect will. I will not partner with fear or shame or hatred or anger because I am a child of trust.

Father, I present my body to you as a living sacrifice, holy and acceptable to you, thanks to Jesus. I trust you, Holy Spirit, to sanctify me, teach me, counsel me, change me, fill me, renew my mind, and make me more like Jesus every day. Fill me completely with you so that I am fully alive to life and truth. Teach me how to discern your voice. Fill me completely so that I always respond to thoughts that are not from you with truth. I can live like God in true righteousness and holiness. Thank you that I am attaining the whole measure of the fullness of Christ. AMEN!

Wait and listen for God's response through your thoughts, feelings, and senses. Write or draw any positive thoughts, mental pictures, feelings, or words God gives you.

MY
SURR-
ENDER

61

NOTES

62

NOTES

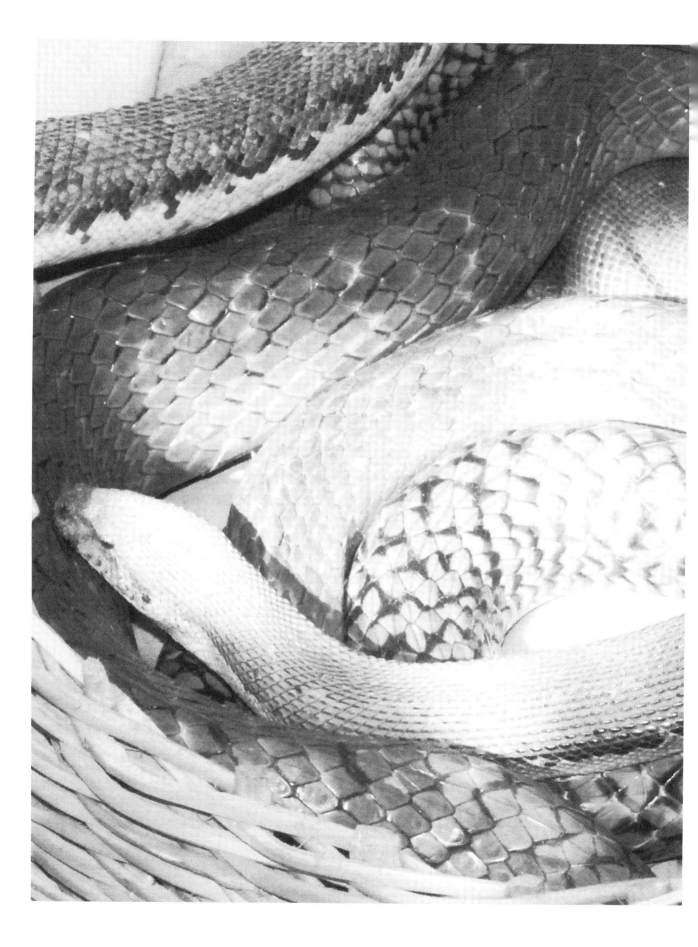

9

THE NATURE OF EVIL

When I was in high school, I became curious about and started exploring New Age practices. In my first semester at college, I began practicing Wicca. It totally drew me in because it was a way to practice spirituality and acknowledge the supernatural that the very traditional church of my childhood seemed to overlook. I learned fast, and it seemed so natural to me that I truly believed I had found my destiny. I saw myself on this spiritual path for the rest of my life. And this was who I was for a little more than three years.

Unbeknownst to me, a newly saved friend started praying for me at his small group meeting. I started having nightmares—not just average nightmares, but intense and very real nightmares. I knew that these dreams were revealing to me that the spiritual path I was on was deadly, and that the goddess that I was choosing to worship hated me and wanted to kill me. I was scared and I didn't know how to fix it. I quit practicing Wicca, but I didn't know what would possibly be big enough to protect me from this murderous goddess and the other gods I had been worshipping. Everything else in my life seemed confusing, and my reality that had felt so right for three years had completely been turned upside-down. I had a lot of bad days.

Every night I hoped that I would make it to the next morning so that I could continue searching for freedom, because I felt very aware of hope for my life. I didn't know what to call it, but I knew it was there. I kept trying to draw it to myself and just tried to be open to it. One night I was driving home from school in that state of confusion when Elton John's "Holy Moses" came on the radio. I thought, Fine! Whatever! I'll go home and read about Moses, *but I really didn't expect that it would do any good.*

Even though there had never been any part of the Bible that I understood to be mine, and I never got the Christian God, I did remember enough about the Bible to know that Moses was toward the front. Upon opening the Bible, the page was on Exodus 3. As good a place to start as any, *I thought. Well, Exodus 3 is the story of Moses in front of the burning bush. God is telling Moses to go to Egypt and to tell Pharaoh to set his people free. Moses asks, "When I go to Egypt, who do I say sent me?" and God's voice answers from the burning bush, "Tell them Yahweh sent you." And with that, I had one of those moments when I felt like a load of bricks fell on me. I knew that this was the name of the hope that I was looking for. I told Jesus that night that I was sorry for rebelling against him and that I would gladly follow him for the rest of my life. I haven't been scared of the goddess since, because in that first encounter I also knew that the God of the Bible was much bigger than the false gods I had been running from.*

—Bonnie

The occult, or anything that comes from an ungodly source, may seem exciting, but it takes hold quickly. We remain unaware of how insidiously evil slips into a life and works from the inside to infect everything else—just like a virus. We find our desire to know God waning, and our quest to live a more exciting life seems paramount. That's the thing about the devil; he has to slither in and do his work on the quiet, slowly erecting a wall between us and God until we're not interested in knowing the Father anymore.

> *From experience he knew that some thoughts left him sad while others made him happy, and little by little he came to perceive the different spirits that were moving him; one coming from the devil, the other coming from God. ~ St. Ignatius of Loyola*

The devil, Satan, the beast—we have many different names for the angel that was kicked out of heaven so many years ago, but who is he? What did he do? What is he up to today?

Satan used to be called Lucifer—an angel of light. His job was to lead the angelic host in continuous praises, and his voice and face were beautiful. His face must have shone with the light of heaven to have such a great name. He was called an "anointed guardian cherub" (Ezek. 28:14). No one knows exactly what happened next, but Isaiah 14 tells us that he said "I will ascend to heaven; above the stars of God. I will set my throne on high […] I will make myself like the Most High" (Isa. 14:13-14). *Obviously not a very smart cookie.*

"The dragon and his angels fought back, but he was defeated, and there was no longer any place for them in heaven. And the great dragon was thrown down, that ancient serpent, who is called the devil and Satan, the deceiver of the whole world—he was thrown down to the earth, and his angels were thrown down with him.

His tail swept down a third of the stars of heaven and cast them to the earth." God kicked him out of heaven. Ezekiel 28:16-17 says: "I cast you as a profane thing from the mountain of God, and I destroyed you, O guardian cherub. You […] corrupted your wisdom for the sake of your splendor. I cast you to the ground."

This tells us a number of things:
1. God is much more powerful than the devil.
2. God always knows what the devil is up to.
3. God is fully capable of kicking the devil out of any place in which he appoints himself ruler.
4. If only one-third of the angels were thrown to earth with the devil, he is already outnumbered two-to-one.

Not only do we have the authority to take down anything the devil does, it is our expected job to do so. We have no reason to be afraid of the devil when we are alive in God!

> *Authority is delegated power. Behind the authority possessed by the believer, there is a Power infinitely greater than that which backs his enemies. ~ Rev. J.A. MacMillan*

REFLECTION

Journal your thoughts on the following points.

- Jesus is the ultimate authority.

- Jesus gave his disciples that authority.

- Jesus not only gave us forgiveness and life via the cross, he also gave us all power and authority.

- Christ was given to us. We are the fullness of Christ's life and power and authority and love.

- God expects us to destroy Satan and his minions.

REFLECTION

The only way Satan can control you is through fear and lies. How do you feel about that? Journal your thoughts here.

TRUTH

What is the truth about evil? Mull over the following Scriptures and write down anything God shows you through them.

"And Jesus came and said to them, 'All authority in heaven and on earth has been given to me'" (Matt. 28:18).

"And he called to him his twelve disciples and gave them authority over unclean spirits, to cast them out, and to heal every disease and every affliction" (Matt. 10:1-3).

"And he put all things under his [Christ's] feet and gave him as head over all things to the church, which is his body, the fullness of him who fills all in all" (Eph. 1:22-23).

"Then comes the end, when he delivers the kingdom to God the Father after destroying every rule and every authority and power [through the authority of his body, the church]" (1 Cor. 15:23-25).

"And the dragon and his angels fought back, but he was defeated, and there was no longer any place for them in heaven" (Rev. 12:7-8).

Personal Prayer

Father, I'm sorry for allowing my mind more time to focus on my fear of the devil and his limited power and limited demons than on your unlimited power and huge angelic force. You've told us to focus on what is good and lovely and truthful, and that's what I choose to do today—I choose to focus on you and your love and your truth. From now on, I will not waste valuable time in my day to focus on a destructive, vicious, lying devil.

Wait and listen for God's response through your thoughts, feelings, and senses. Write or draw any positive thoughts, mental pictures, feelings, or words God gives you.

NOTES

70

NOTES

10
THE POWER OF A LIE v. THE TRUTH

For years as an assistant youth pastor, I felt like I was never good enough. On bad days I felt like a total failure. I didn't see very many conversions. I saw few kids really go deep and stay strong. Some just walked away, or worse yet, faked it and took others down with them. Most graduated and either disappeared or faded out of our lives. Typically if I heard about one, it wasn't that good. There were a few "success stories," but not many.

I seemed to be in minor trouble on a regular basis with a pastor, an elder, or parents. When I looked at myself, I didn't see the qualities, gifts, or level of wisdom I saw in the youth pastors I admired and considered effective. I would remind myself that this was what I was made for, but on too many days I just muddled through.

It was hard. It was essentially impossible.

As so often happens, God finally got me to see the reality of truths I had been telling the students. Comparison is generally a really bad idea. I wasn't made to be those other guys, to reach the kids they reached. It really, truly was okay that I mostly tilled ground, planted, watered, and fertilized—someone had to! Eventually I started hearing back from some who had moved away, how I had made a huge difference just by loving them and believing in them when they felt no one else did. Some of them are doing great, some are hanging on by a thread, but they haven't given up. Some come back for more.

I was so busy believing I had to be someone else, I lost sight of who I was. When I started seeing myself the way God does, and then seeing the youth as he does—made in his image, forgiven, redeemed—I knew I was no longer a failure. I'm God's son. And it's not my job to fix or save anyone, just love them and offer them the good news in all its glorious forms.

Suddenly, it was easy.

—Miles

Our Creator makes absolute perfection when he makes a child, and even in the womb his presence and love are constant. Even there, however, the devil tries to crack those walls of safety by using the only two things he has—fear and lies. Babies are very perceptive to their immediate and extended environments; they can hear fighting and feel fear and pain. Sometimes this will be through osmosis from the mother, or it will be a reaction to external stimuli. It is quite normal for a baby then, even in utero, to experience a crack in his defense system and allow a lie to come in.

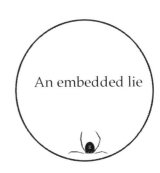

Perfect beginnings   A crack in the system   An embedded lie

That lie gets in there and stays there until it is replaced with truth.

All through childhood, more and more lies worm their way in. Some of us had great childhoods—loving functional parents, good friends, a safe environment, and all our needs met. For others, the opposite is true. The pain we feel today, though, is not just related to our level of pain and trauma in childhood; it's also directly related to the number of lies we hold onto as adults. There is no bonus to seeing life through a dirty lens, even if it feels more real.

The good news is that we are now fully alive in God, we live in the presence of the Holy Spirit at all times, and we have all of God's truth at our disposal. The lies may be triggered regularly, but we know that's all that's going on—and God's truth will overcome the lies.

"And I heard a loud voice in heaven, saying, 'Now the salvation and the power and the kingdom of our God and the authority of his Christ have come, for the accuser of our brothers has been thrown down, who accuses them day and night before our God" (Rev. 12).

"The thief comes only to steal and kill and destroy. I came that they may have life and have it abundantly" (John 10:10). In order to obey Christ, we must consistently agree with his truth and not with Satan's lies. The only way to know God's truth is to know everything the Bible says about you. While the devil may consistently try to accuse you of things and try to make you withdraw in shame, the enemy talking to you does not mean you are not free. You're already free and forgiven, but the devil doesn't like to give up easily. As you keep responding with more truth, however, the enemy will eventually get tired of his blood on your sword.

REFLECTION

Check every lie (below) that feels true, even if in your head you know it isn't.

AFRAID	ABANDONED	ASHAMED & GUILTY
I'm afraid that something bad is going to happen. I'm afraid of death or dying. I'm afraid of emotional pain, breakdown or physical pain. If I trust, I will get hurt. It is just a matter of time before something bad happens again. I can't make a decision or something will go wrong. I'm afraid of missing out on something good.	I am abandoned. I am not needed by anyone. I am all alone. I will always be by myself. There is no one to protect me. God has forsaken me. No one will believe me. I have been betrayed by everyone. I don't matter to anyone. If I did, I wouldn't be alone.	What happened was my fault. I made others do the things they did. I deserved it. I was a participant. I should have known better. I should have told someone. It happened because of my looks, my gender, or my body. I did not try to run away. I kept going back.

STAINED	HOPELESS	POWERLESS
I am dirty, shameful, evil, or perverted because of what happened to me. My life is ruined. I will never feel clean again. Everyone can see my shame, filth, or dirtiness. I will always be hurt or damaged because of what has happened. I can never be the same.	It is never going to get any better. There is no way out. There is no good thing for me. I have no reason to live. The only option I have is death. There are no options available to me. There is nothing that I can do.	I know what needs to be done, but I am powerless to do it. I need to take care of things or people, but I can't. I can't resist. I am overwhelmed. I don't have what it takes to make it stop. Everything is out of control. I am too small, weak, or helpless to do anything.

WORTHLESS
I am unlovable. I am not needed. I am worthless. I don't matter. I was a mistake and I should have never been born. I am in the way. Girls are less important than boys. Boys are less important than girls. God could never love or accept me. I am defective. There is something wrong with me. I'm not pretty, smart, athletic, or talented enough. I'll never be as good as _____.

Talk to the Father about these lies that feel true, and write down his response.

TRUTH

What is the truth about you? Mull over the following Scriptures and write down anything God shows you through them.

MY CHILD

You may not know me, but I know everything about you. Ps. 139:1
I know when you sit down and when you rise up. Ps. 139:2
I am familiar with all your ways. Ps. 139:3
Even the very hairs on your head are numbered. Matt. 10:29-31
For you were made in my image. Gen. 1:27
For you are my offspring. Acts 17:28

I knew you before you were conceived. Jer. 1:4-5
I chose you when I planned creation. Eph. 1:11-12
You were not a mistake, all your days are written in my book. Ps. 139:15-16
I determined the exact time of your birth and where you would live. Acts 17:26
You are fearfully and wonderfully made. Ps. 139:14
I knit you together in your mother's womb. Ps. 139:13
And brought you forth on the day you were born. Ps. 71:6

It is my desire to lavish my love on you. 1 John 3:1
Simply because you are my child and I am your father. 1 John 3:1
I offer you more than your earthly father ever could. Matt. 7:11
For I am the perfect father. Matt. 5:48

My plan for your future has always been filled with hope. Jer. 29:11
Because I love you with an everlasting love. Jer. 31:3
My thoughts of you are countless as the sand on the seashore. Ps. 139:17-18
And I rejoice over you with singing. Zeph. 3:17
I will never stop doing good to you. Jer. 32:40
For you are my treasured possession. Exod. 19:5
I desire to establish you with all my heart and all my soul. Jer. 32:41
And I want to show you great and marvelous things. Jer. 33:3
Delight in me and I will give you the desires of your heart. Ps. 37:4
For it is I who gave you those desires. Phil. 2:13

I am your greatest encourager. 2 Thess. 2:16-17
I am also the Father who comforts you in all your troubles. 2 Cor. 1:3-4
When you are brokenhearted, I am close to you. Ps. 34:18
As a shepherd carries a lamb, I have carried you close to my heart. Isa. 40:11
One day I will wipe away every tear from your eyes. Rev. 21:3-4
And I'll take away all the pain you have suffered on this earth. Rev. 21:3-4

I am your Father and I love you even as I love my son, Jesus. John 17:23
For in Jesus, my love for you is revealed. John 17:26
He came to demonstrate that I am for you, not against you. Rom. 8:31
And to tell you that I am not counting your sins. 2 Cor. 5:18-19

Jesus died so that you and I could be reconciled. 2 Cor. 5:18-19
His death was the ultimate expression of my love for you. 1 John 4:10
I gave up everything I loved that I might gain your love. Rom. 8:31-32
If you receive the gift of my son Jesus, you receive me. 1 John 2:23
And nothing will ever separate you from my love again. Rom. 8:38-39

Come home and I'll throw the biggest party heaven has ever seen. Luke 15:7
I have always been Father, and will always be Father. Eph. 3:14-15
My question is, "Will you be my child?" John 1:12-13
I am waiting for you. Luke 15:11-32

Love, your Dad, Almighty God
Adapted from the Father's Love Letter

REFLECTION

Talk to the Father about his truths that disagree with your lies, and write down or draw his response.

PERSONAL PRAYER

Father, there are a number of lies that feel true to me—lies about you and lies about me—but your truth declares otherwise. You are good and kind and you adore me. I am your perfect creation and I am the amazing recipient of all that you are. I don't need to look at myself and my life through a dirty lens when the view is so spectacular at your side.

That's what I want from now on, Father, I want to see everything the way you do. Thank you for making that possible.

Wait and listen for God's response through your thoughts, feelings, and senses. Write or draw any positive thoughts, mental pictures, feelings, or words God gives you.

NOTES

78

NOTES

11
MY DISCONNECTING

I was always good at disappearing as a kid. I'd either disappear into the world of the latest book in my hands, or I'd let my mind wander off so I could be anywhere but in the current moment. I don't know why I automatically went there so often.

Perhaps it was safer in a world of my own making—one in which I was the ruler of my domain, a world that no one else could come into and ruin with harsh words or rejecting body language. But while it was a great way for a child to create a mental safety net, it was not the place to camp out in in the real world. The moment I started a job, my inability to live in the moment meant that a lot of people were not served in love. I was serving myself and avoiding the needs of those around me, because I was unable to focus on the job at hand.

It took a lot of work and time with my Father to shake off the habit, and while I still cannot claim that I am always mentally present and focused in every conversation and moment, I don't feel that need for personal safety anymore. I can rest in God in the moment, and my mental safety is automatic.

—Sally

We all shut down or withdraw in one way or another. We all want to feel safe. We don't want to be in the room with people who create an atmosphere of fear or pain, so we stop talking or daydream or disappear to the point that our bodies may be present, but nothing else is. For many of us, withdrawal has become so automatic that we use it to drown out boring conversations or to shut down our emotions when we are doing something we have no energy for. We do it when we become tired of fighting or engaging or hoping. There is no life in withdrawal.

Dissociation:

The disconnection or separation of something from something else or the state of being disconnected.

Chemistry the splitting of a molecule into smaller molecules, atoms, or ions, especially by a reversible process.

Psychiatry separation of normally related mental processes, resulting in one group functioning independently from the rest (*The Oxford English Dictionary*, online edition).

In other words, the state of not being whole or complete. *When you choose to withdraw and shut down, choosing to not be fully present in each moment of the day, everyone loses.*

> Eli was the father of two grown men who dishonored the Lord in numerous ways. Eli's role was one of responsibility: he had the job of presenting the sins of Israel before the Lord and offering a sacrifice for them. Sin was a big deal to God, but Eli withdrew and ignored his sons' ongoing decisions to flaunt their sin in the face of God, when it was Eli's job to resist and oppose it. With his withdrawal, he ended up being the enabler of their sin, and that enabling made him guilty of neglect. (See 1 Sam. 2-4.)

So far, we have talked about how to walk in freedom, in truth, and in wholeness. We've learned of new ways to respond to trauma and emotional pain, and it's been deep and freeing—but perhaps despite all the steps we have worked through so far, it is still a natural habit to shut down certain memories in order to not feel their pain. While this may have been a huge help in childhood, it is not the path to maturity. Shutting down causes those around us to feel neglected, uncared for, and unsupported. It stops us from living responsible lives, from being fully present in every moment. We are now adults, and Jesus doesn't need us to use coping mechanisms anymore because he has made a new way.

If something triggers disconnection, don't then move into the shadows, alone with your thoughts. Spend your time with friends and in worship, or even just with people who care about you. It might feel more self-protective to isolate yourself, but the reality is that you need to let the light in. God wants to walk straight into our lives and be our center. He wants us to be his holy habitation, his sanctuary. We can't be a fully functional sanctuary for others until we are whole, and we can't be whole until we stop shutting down.

One of the greatest gifts you can give God, yourself, and others is your presence.

REFLECTION

Understand that this is just a first step for people who struggle with this type of living on a daily basis.

Imagine you are an unmade jigsaw. Each piece of the jigsaw represents a different method of self-protection you use to handle fear or pain—one might get angry, another might hide, another might eat too much or too little, another might practice self-harm. List some of the things you do below.

Invite Jesus to join each piece of you, and through highlighting each method of self-protection, talk to him about your fears and concerns of losing your familiar habits and having nothing to replace them with. Talk to him about, for example, your fear of having to interact with people until each discussion is over rather than hoping and pretending it goes away.

Then step into Jesus with all your self-protective pieces with their memories and behaviors, and rest there until you sense your oneness with him. *If this is difficult, remember that Jesus died so that you could be one with him, and so that he could take care of your memories, fears, and pain, and all the ways you try to cover them up. He is safe.*

Write about this experience.

TRUTH

What is the truth about disconnecting? Mull over the following Scriptures and write down anything God shows you through them.

"[Caiaphas] prophesied that Jesus would die for the nation, and not for the nation only, but also to gather into one the children of God who are scattered abroad" (John 11:51-52).

"Holy Father, keep them in your name, which you have given me, that they may be one, even as we are one" (John 17:11).

"I pray also for those who will believe in me … that all of them may be one, Father, just as you are in me and I am in you. May they also be in us so that the world may believe that you have sent me. I have given them the glory that you gave me, that they may be one as we are one: I in them and you in me" (John 17:20-23).

"I am the voice of one crying out in the wilderness, 'Make straight the way of the Lord,' as the prophet Isaiah said" (John 1:23).

"Do nothing from selfishness or empty conceit, but with humility of mind regard one another as more important than yourselves; do not merely look out for your own personal interests, but also for the interests of others" (Phil. 2:3-4).

Personal prayer

Thank you, Father, for helping me to be whole and free. Thank you for choosing me to be your temple, a home for the Holy Spirit, and thank you for helping me to keep stretching so that you have a better fit in every area of my mind, will, and emotions.

Thank you that I can honor the moments of each day and the moments you give me with others by giving them my full attention. Thank you that you are my place of safety, and I can become that place of safety for others.

Wait and listen for God's response through your thoughts, feelings, and senses. Write or draw any positive thoughts, mental pictures, feelings, or words God gives you.

NOTES

NOTES

87

CHRIST'S CHARACTER – THE PROCESS

12

I realized that I had a problem with judging others even before I knew Jesus. One day after high school, I was at the mall by myself. For the most part, I was too good for the mall—everything was so unoriginal and preppy and I was all about nonconformity, but this was one of the rare occasions when I was there. A couple of frat-looking guys (whom I was also too good for, because those *people were, of course, sooooo snobby) walked by and tried to say hello. I looked the other way and ignored them. I heard one of them say, "Wow, what a snob!" Yeah, that was a wake-up call for sure!*

At the age of twenty, I started following Jesus and, oddly enough, probably went backward when I tried to define others' sins for them so that they could see how much they needed Jesus. Becoming less judgmental has been a process brought on by others (mostly Christians and family—ouch!) making horribly incorrect assumptions about me and my motivations. That has been a hard lesson in how I have come to not be so uptight about other people and to give them the benefit of the doubt, or at least participate in conversations and questions instead of judging their lives. Hopefully I now help them to feel loved and able to see themselves as lovable. I have learned to do this because I know it is how I would like to be treated.

—Bonnie

I prayed the "sinner's prayer" when I was five. You'd think that with receiving all of Jesus at such a young age, his presence would have prevented all the things I did that did not reflect his holiness through the years that followed. But that was not the case, and that's because some internal lies screamed louder than his love, and I believed them. Pain always seeks pleasure, and I sought out acceptance and validation as my drugs of choice. Getting that through unhealthy sources meant that the very things I was seeking turned into my captors, feeding me for a few minutes and then mocking me when I crawled back for more.

We all have learned and adapted unhealthy ways of dealing with pain or difficulties—withdrawal or self-imposed isolation, hard-heartedness, self-pity, a victim mentality, addictions, anger, judgmentalism, abuse—but we can't blame any of them on other people. We respond in these ways because we are allowing our lies to be triggered and we haven't taken the time to live in the truth. Rather than choose truth, we repeat old habits of self-protection because we fear that the pain of the truth will be too much to bear. We believe that self-protection and pleasure leads to freedom.

While denial is sometimes a God-given gift that helps us to survive until we are ready, a life of faith is also a life of truth. We need to choose a new path. The path to sanctification and freedom only comes through living in faith—one thought, one choice, one step at a time.

> Joseph had an ongoing sanctification process to live through. While he was close to God in his early years, and he obviously heard him clearly, he then went through many trials that would have tempted him to believe lies over truth. He was abandoned, betrayed, invalidated, afraid, and powerless; yet he chose to turn every step of discouragement into an opportunity to grow. Because of that, he ended up saving his family and the future of Israel. (Read Gen. 37-50.)

Inner healing, cleansing, and purifying are parts of the sanctification process. Sanctification refers to being stretched into our new nature, being active in the image and nature of Jesus with our unique skins on. It's not that Jesus hasn't made us holy through the cross; it's that we are intent on receiving so much of him that we need to get rid of everything that is not truth to make room. We are all being made pure in thought, word, and deed in God.

Blaming others for your weaknesses will never make you strong.

Jesus wants us whole. Jesus wants us pure. Jesus wants us powerful. We can only be all those things when we live in truth and in the ongoing sanctification process of surrender, receiving all of him, and obedience.

REFLECTION

Write your responses to each of the following questions:

What is God sanctifying, consecrating, or making holy in me right now?

What area of difficulty in my life is God using to help me grow more into him?

How has God used my past experiences to stretch me into my new nature?

REFLECTION

Are there any unhealthy, self-protective patterns I see myself reverting to?

When I talk to God about those, what is his response?

TRUTH

What is the truth about becoming like Jesus? Mull over the following Scriptures and write down anything God shows you through them.

"Now may the God of peace himself sanctify (to make holy; i.e. purify or consecrate) you completely (whole-complete, through and through; absolutely perfect--draws attention to the several parts which constitute a person); and may your whole (complete in every part; perfectly sound, entire) spirit (pneuma--a current of air, rational and immortal soul) and soul (psuche breath spirit, life) and body (soma, the body as a sound whole) be kept (to guard--from loss or injury; prob. by keeping the eyes upon) blameless (without blame, faultlessly) at (indicating the point reached or entered) the coming (a being near, to be near, presence) of our Lord Jesus Christ. He who calls you is faithful; he will surely do it" (I Thes. 5:23; Amplified Bible).

"Sanctify them in the truth; your word is truth" (John 17:17).

"Beloved, I pray that all may go well with you and that you may be in good health (Hugiaino: healthy, sound, in good health--whole), as it goes well with your soul" (3 John 1:2; Amplified Bible).

"The testing of your faith produces steadfastness. And let steadfastness have its full effect, that you may be perfect and complete, lacking in nothing" (James 1:2-8).

PERSONAL PRAYER

Father, I'm sorry for choosing to respond in an unhealthy way when my lies are triggered. From now on, I choose to run to you so that the lies can be exposed and your truth can reign. Help me learn how to be whole and free so I can respond with nothing but love from now on, no matter who I am with or what circumstances I am facing. Thank you for the trials I go through because they give me an opportunity to grow into steadfastness, perfection, completion, and wholeness. Please give me the wisdom you give so generously so that I can live in you this way every day. Amen.

Wait and listen for God's response through your thoughts, feelings, and senses. Write or draw any positive thoughts, mental pictures, feelings, or words God gives you.

NOTES

NOTES

13 BLESSINGS AND CURSES

In the early days of my walk with God, I was very much against any establishment bent on hell. Every time I went by a place of worship to another god(s), or by a store that stripped the value of women to one thing, I would begin to grumble and groan in my spirit. I'd launch into rebuking mode, attacking every ungodly thing they were doing in prayer. Until one day I opened my mouth to do the same thing outside a Buddhist temple, and I heard God say, "Lyn, how long are you going to keep cursing them? That's what you're doing—releasing the judgment in your heart over them. Was it my judgment that brought you to me or my love? What gives you the liberty to curse them when I want to bless them?"

I was shocked, but I knew he was right, because I am not God. I just didn't know how to go about doing the exact opposite of what I was used to doing, so I asked him for guidance. He said, "You're creative; think about it."

I looked at how I was to have the mind and character of Christ, so I thought about what he did and began to release the kindness of God and a revelation of who he is over those very same institutions I had previously cursed. The very first time I prayed a blessing of God's kindness over a Buddhist temple, I felt his power. Something hit the atmosphere over it that shook the place in the spirit realm. As I continued to pray over places, I added the blessing of the revelation of true intimacy with the Father.

I started to see results—one of the video stores I had been cursing for years closed down after just one year of releasing blessing. Even in my own life, I was able to see more clearly how God sees others, and when I released blessing, my wounding or anger toward sin went away because I wasn't tied to it anymore.

—Lyn

CURSE

"1 : a prayer or invocation for harm or injury to come upon one; 2 : something that is cursed or accursed; 3 : evil or misfortune that comes as if in response to oath or as retribution; 4 : a cause of great harm or misfortune" (www.merri-am-webster.com).

> THE OLD LIFE with curses: "Just as sin came into the world through one man, and death through sin, and so death spread to all men because all sinned" (Rom. 5:12).

BLESSING

"1a : the act or words of one that blesses; b : approval, encouragement; 2 : a thing conducive to happiness or welfare" (www.merriam-webster.com).

> THE NEW LIFE with blessings: "Christ redeemed us from the curse of the law by becoming a curse for us—for it is written, 'Cursed is everyone who is hanged on a tree'" (Gal 3:13).

God was the only one in the Old Testament with the power to curse according to his Law, and we are now free from every curse of the Law. Jesus cursed only one thing—the fig tree, saying, "Let no fruit grow on you ever again," and the fig tree withered (Mt. 21:19; Mark 11:14). He also spoke about curses from people. In the only reference in the New Testament, when he tells us what to do if someone curses us, Jesus said, "Bless those who curse you, and pray for those who spitefully use you" (Luke 6:28).

Living under a curse all depends on which standard you live by—the standard of the cross or the Law. If you live by the Law, you will be cursed by the Law, because no human can fulfill it perfectly. "For all who rely on works of the law are under a curse; for it is written, 'Cursed be everyone who does not abide by all things written in the Book of the Law, and do them'" (Gal. 3:9-10).

Living under God's blessing is simple: "Now it is evident that no one is justified before God by the law, for 'The righteous shall live by faith'" (Gal.3). We live in the freedom of the finished work.

Whatever you are afraid of will be your biggest authority.

We can't suffer the effects of someone else's curse when we live in the blessing, but any lie/any spirit can come into our spirit if we open the door to it. The battle is in the mind; the power is in the credence we give to a thought, a fear, a lie. The power is not in the curse.

So you're saying that if I'm having a hard time in life, it's because my faith is not strong enough? No! But evil increases substantially through fear and lies. The less of a fear-filled environment we give evil, the less evil can triumph. The more we fill our environment with love and hope, the more good triumphs. James seemed to recognize this. He didn't say: "Whenever you have a hard time, it's because someone in your generational history sinned and now you're the one suffering." He said: "Count it all joy, my brothers, when you meet trials of various kinds, for you know that the testing of your faith produces steadfastness. And let steadfastness have its full effect, that you may be perfect and complete, lacking in nothing" (James 1:2-8).

So why is it that my family line seems to suffer so much more than other families? Every family has habits and ways of seeing life that have invited dysfunction and pain, e.g., witchcraft, the occult, addictions, mental problems, sexual problems, religious restrictions, sickness and diseases, emotional disorders, death. Family habits usually repeat themselves, so if control and anger are present in one generation, they will more than likely be repeated in the subsequent generations. The same goes for ways of dealing with memories—abuse and illegitimacy will usually repeat themselves when an environment was created in the home for certain demons to feel welcome, and demons are always looking for ways to fill a soul with lies so they can control outcomes to their satisfaction.

What we do is take what we see and hear and start to doubt God. We begin to think about dying at the same age as our mothers of a certain sickness, or we think that because our father was an abuser, we will end up abusing others, or we assume that because Mom was depressed, we will be too. I'm guilty. We all are.

If you look at things from God's perspective, fear is no longer a major factor in our thinking. Once we get rid of the fear and the lies and start putting some great new ways of living into practice, our family history can be a nonissue.

If we are to be like Jesus, then we are to bless those who curse us and love with his kind of love. We choose to see those who have hurt us through the lens of love and we pray for them and bless them with our words, both in public *and* in private. We can choose to be unaffected by the words of others. We can choose to be free. Let's walk out of fear and into victory.

REFLECTION

A sample blessing to pray over those who curse you can go like this priestly blessing used to bless the people of Israel: *The Lord bless you and keep you; the Lord make his face to shine upon you and give you peace.* We know we have truly forgiven someone when we can bless him. Write down the names of those you would like to bless instead of curse today.

REFLECTION

Talk to God about any family history you have been afraid of repeating or suffering from. Write his response below.

TRUTH

What is the truth about God's blessing and other people's curses? Mull over the following Scriptures and write down anything that God might be showing you through them.

"And Balak said to Balaam, 'What have you done to me? I took you to curse my enemies, and behold, you have done nothing but bless them.' And he answered and said, 'Must I not take care to speak what the Lord puts in my mouth?'" (Num. 22-24.).

"I will bless you and make your name great, so that you will be a blessing [...] in you all the families of the earth shall be blessed" (Gen. 12:2-3).

"You shall not curse the people, for they are blessed" (Num. 22:12).

"I know that he whom you bless is blessed, and he whom you curse is cursed" (Num. 22:6).

"And God blessed them [...] And God blessed them [...] Male and female he created them, and he blessed them" (Gen. 1:22,28; 5:2).

Personal prayer

Lord, I refuse to be double-minded from now on. Let me mark today down as the day when I choose to live from a place of victory. Instead of allowing thoughts and words that can curse others, I choose to bless every single person who has ever wounded me. Today I speak blessings and life over (write names below):

Wait and listen for God's response through your thoughts, feelings, and senses. Write or draw any positive thoughts, mental pictures, feelings, or words God gives you.

NOTES

NOTES

14

MY UNHEALTHY ATTACHMENTS

I dated a man on and off for three years. Every time we broke up, it was because he had told me yet another lie or made me feel less important than other friends and relationships in his life. No matter what we did to try to talk about it afterward, he always managed to turn it back on me. I knew the relationship wasn't healthy, but invariably something would happen to put him in a place of need and we'd start dating again. I knew I was being codependent, I knew I was enabling his lies and disconnection and lack of boundaries with others, but there was this strong attachment to him that kept pulling me back.

I finally went to someone for some one-on-one prayer, and in that time Jesus kept drawing me close to him with much love and affection and compassion. He understood my need for connection and my need to feel needed, but at the same time, he was letting me know that I had him and he was enough. It was time to move on, and he gave me the strength to let go. —Sue

An unhealthy attachment: any connection that does not give you the freedom to be yourself. Soul attachments can be ties to the mind, will, and emotions of another person or attachments to such things as drugs, electronics, or work. Ungodly soul attachments of the mind, will, and emotions begin when we think we need another person or thing in order to be whole.

Human love cannot rescue people from their weaknesses, failures, hurts, and sorrows; God can not only meet their needs, but also more than compensate for a lack of love from others. We cannot judge his love insufficient. ~ Joyce Strong

We have different levels of attachment to others, and we can compare them thus:
> THREAD: A casual connection – an easy tie to break
> STRING: A regular connection, like one with an acquaintance with whom you share common interests – takes a bit of effort to break
> ROPE: A close connection, like one with a good friend with whom you are somewhat vulnerable – requires a lot of effort to break, especially if tension exists
> CABLE: Usually a connection with a close relative or daily habit – requires a lot of deliberate force to break and can affect the soul

God has designed us to have healthy attachments, and we can see that in his design for marriage, in the relationship between Ruth and Naomi, in the friendship of David and Jonathan, in the loyalty of David's men, and in the unity of the body of Christ.

A healthy tie begins with a healthy perspective (see Matt 6:33). God asks us to come to him with our pain instead of bringing people to him so that he will fix them for us. We want him to bless so many unhealthy attachments that do not give us life; instead they drag us down and distract us from our relationship with God. We focus on past memories or have emotional ties to things or music or money; we nurse memories of an old flame; we feed old grudges and wounds; we won't "leave and cleave"; we won't let go of the dead or of friendships that have died; we won't let our kids grow up and be independent; we won't break free of control or anger or compromise; we keep dating father or mother figures. In a nutshell, unhealthy attachments to something or someone causes a (sometimes obsessive) preoccupation with another while neglecting the things on God's heart.

Physical connections have far more power at times than emotional ones, from that first kiss to the final act. The sexual acts that cause ungodly ties, though, are the ones done outside of marriage that invade the spirit—intercourse, oral sex, and pornography, among others.

In the same way that lies implant themselves into our souls once we choose to believe them, ungodly spirits cross natural spiritual boundaries and implant themselves into our spirits when we participate in physical relationships outside of marriage. By doing so, we provide an open door to the ungodly spirits in another person. Only prayer can cut those ties and send those spirits back where they came from.

REFLECTION

Wait on God and ask him who you are still connected to in an unhealthy way. Write their names below, followed by the strength of that connection—thread, string, rope, or cable. (We will pray through those attachments later in this chapter.)

Ask the Father if there is anything else he would like to show you about those attachments. Write his response below.

REFLECTION

Ask the Father whom you have healthy attachments to and write their names below.

TRUTH

What is the truth about unhealthy attachments? Mull over the following Scriptures and write down anything that God might be showing you through them.

"Therefore a man shall leave his father and his mother and hold fast to his wife, and they shall become one flesh" (Gen. 2:21-24).

"May the LORD do so to me and more also if anything but death parts me from you" (Ruth 1:14-17).

"As soon as he had finished speaking to Saul, the soul of Jonathan was knit to the soul of David, and Jonathan loved him as his own soul" (1 Sam. 18:1).

"I appeal to you, brothers, by the name of our Lord Jesus Christ, that all of you agree, and that there be no divisions among you, but that you be united in the same mind and the same judgment" (1 Cor. 1:10).

"So all the men of Israel withdrew from David and followed Sheba the son of Bichri. But the men of Judah followed their king steadfastly from the Jordan to Jerusalem" (2 Sam. 20:2).

PERSONAL PRAYER
PRAYER TO BREAK SOUL ATTACHMENTS
Insert names where appropriate:

Father, I am sorry for playing any part in causing a relationship to be unhealthy. In the name of Jesus Christ I now reject, cut off, and release myself from all ungodly soul attachments and unhealthy bonds with the following people _____
_____.

Please break me of all of my tendencies to: obsessive preoccupations, domination, control, passivity, apathy, unforgiveness, anger, blame, accusations, fear, and intimidation in relationships. I declare every demonic hold in my life that has come as a result of unhealthy soul attachments null and void. I renounce the lie that my life is not complete if these relationships end, and I embrace the truth that all I need is in you, God. I trust you to bring healthy relationships into my life, and to restore all my relationships to good health. I command any and all ungodly connections to be severed, and for anything ungodly that may have entered my soul in our time together to leave my spirit, soul, and body in Jesus's name.

PRAYER TO BREAK SEXUAL ATTACHMENTS
Insert names where appropriate:

Father, I am sorry for being one half of an ungodly physical relationship. I sinned, breaking my promise to live in the fullness of righteousness with you. I repent of all obsession and fascination of sex, and I repent of denying the magnitude of the damage of extramarital sex. (If you were abused: I forgive _____ *for abusing his/her role of authority and for violating my trust.) In the name of Jesus Christ I now reject, break, and loose myself from all ungodly soul and spirit attachments with the following people* _____.

Please break me of all of my tendencies to disobey your standards in relationships. I declare every demonic hold in my life that has come as a result of unhealthy sexual attachments null and void. I renounce all lies that my life is not complete if these relationships end, and I embrace the truth that all I need is in you, God. I trust you to bring healthy relationships into my life, and to restore all my relationships to good health. I command any and all ungodly connections to be severed, and for anything ungodly that may have entered my soul and spirit in our time together to leave my spirit, soul, and body in Jesus's name.

I release _____ *from all of my thoughts, and I choose to now see them through your eyes—as your children, free to be righteous and holy in all their ways.*

NOTES

FOLLOW UP: Give healing some time. Learn who the safe people are and stay in their positive, healthy environment.

NOTES

110

NOTES

15
My Connections to Evil

When I was in my teens, I had a hunger for the power of God. I was a Christian, and had been reading my Bible since I was ten years old, but I was drawn to prophecy and knew that the supernatural side of the Holy Spirit was not smiled upon in my church. As a result, I slowly began to train myself on New Age materials, and I visited many psychics and mediums. I became adept at a number of occult practices. I also became more and more mentally ill, to the point that I went from the top of my class to dropping out of school and locking myself in my bedroom for most of three years. The torment was severe, and although there were other causes of my collapse, related to my upbringing, the real downward spiral did not occur until I became involved in occult practices.

One day, the tormenting thoughts of suicide and despair were too much for me. I had been agoraphobic for quite some time, and also struggled with anorexia and bulimia. My hair was falling out. I wanted to die. I opened my Bible and cried out to God, saying, "Lord, I need help, you have to help me, I can't do this anymore. I can't live like this." The Bible fell open to Deuteronomy 18:10-11: "There shall not be found among you anyone who makes his son or his daughter pass through the fire, or one who practices witchcraft, or a soothsayer, or one who interprets omens, or a sorcerer, or one who conjures spells, or a medium, or a spiritist, or one who calls up the dead."

Conviction came upon me, with great fear and sorrow. I stared at the ceiling and said, "Lord, is this me? Is what I'm doing wrong? Am I evil?" At that moment, I felt a great tension enter the air of my bedroom. I don't know how to explain it, except to say that it was a tangible presence of Light and Darkness. I could feel the darkness in the air become agitated. The tension increased; it felt like lightning was going to strike, and then a figurine that was on top of my TV flew across the room and hit the opposite wall. Every hair on my body went on end, and I knew that God had spoken to me and that the demons were not happy. Up until this point I was hoping that I was communicating with angels. I stood corrected.

I fell to my face and repented with tears, and the Holy Spirit came and comforted me. "What do I do?" I asked. I heard the Lord reply in my head, "Get rid of everything to do with witchcraft. Then obey my voice. Whatever I tell you to do, do."

From that moment I was empowered to break free of the bondages I was under. It was the start of a very trying process of freedom and deliverance, but today I stand free.

—Dusty

In the setting of occult activity, the dominant way of ruling over the members is through vows, blood rituals, and physical acts. If you have ever been a part of any type of ritual, ceremony, or act that did not bring glory to God and his light and truth, then you need to separate yourself from those ungodly attachments.

The devil knows the power of blood and of sexual attachments, but we know the power of the blood of Jesus and of the righteousness that comes through faith in his ultimate power. We have the blessing of being able to receive more of heaven through God's many anointed people, but we are never to receive anything from those "anointed" by another source.

> The Israelites finally escaped from Egypt and their centuries of slavery, and they didn't just get out with the clothes on their backs; they walked out with loads of gold and silver jewelry that the Egyptians had gladly given them just to see the back of them. Merely forty-four days later they reached Mount Sinai, and a few weeks later somehow managed to melt all their jewelry and turn it into an idol because they got tired of waiting for Moses to come back down the mountain. That was the group that never made it to the Promised Land. (Read Ex. 32.)

It's telling that even the Israelites had a problem with patience, a problem with waiting on God to fulfill all their expectations, a problem with hoping in the promises of God, a problem with rushing back to everything familiar, even though those were connections to the very things that had held them captive for so long. The treasure they had taken with them as plunder, as a blessing from God, was turned back into their captor *by choice*.

Just like the attachments that are formed through relationships, so ties are also formed through participation with the occult. In order to be free of anything that has secured itself to your spirit and soul, you need to send it back where it came from and sever all ties with it. It's not that there's a curse or evil stuck to you and you can't get rid of it unless you say the magic words (pun intended); it's that when you form a covenant with someone, you need to annul the covenant in order to move forward in total freedom.

On a wedding day, the bride says, "I promise to love you unconditionally until death parts us." She tells those watching that she "receives" this man. She holds out her hand so that he can place the symbol of comitment on her finger—a sign to show the world that she has committed herself to staying true to her promise. Society will hold her to that, and legal steps have to be taken to annul the promises made. The ring is returned or sold. Property is divided. All signs of connection are dismantled and sent back to the giver. The same thing must happen when we annul our covenants with evil—all signs of connection must be dismantled, all tangible symbols destroyed, all open doors of the heart closed tight. When we step into Jesus, we step into the purest, whitest, clearest beauty one can imagine. Nothing should sully that place of holy intimacy.

Jesus left his grave clothes in the tomb for a reason.

REFLECTION

Think of any time when you made a pact or vow or went through with a ritual, ceremony, or act that did not glorify God or did not bring you into a place of greater intimacy with God. Write them down below.

REFLECTION

Since the time you stepped into the love of God and became one with him, how has your connection to the past become an obstacle to your future relationship with your Father?

Is there anything tangible or spiritual you need to send back to the giver, or that you need to destroy?

Is there anything you need to close your heart to?

Talk to God about these things, and ask him for his persepective. Wait and listen for his response, and write or draw what he says or shows you.

TRUTH

What is the truth about partnering with evil? Mull over the following Scriptures and write down anything that God might be showing you through them.

"There shall not be found among you anyone who burns his son or his daughter as an offering, anyone who practices divination or tells fortunes or interprets omens, or a sorcerer or a charmer or a medium or a necromancer or one who inquires of the dead" (Deut. 18:10-11).

"For what partnership have righteousness and lawlessness, or what fellowship has light with darkness? Or what harmony has Christ with Belial, or [...] what agreement has the temple of God with idols? For we are the temple of the living God" (2 Cor. 6:14-16).

"'Come out from their midst and be separate,' says the Lord.'And do not touch what is unclean'" (2 Cor. 6:17).

"Finally, all of you, have unity of mind [...] Do not repay evil for evil or reviling for reviling, but on the contrary, bless, for to this you were called. [...] Let him keep his tongue from evil and his lips from speaking deceit; let him turn away from evil and do good; let him seek peace and pursue it. For the eyes of the Lord are on the righteous" (1 Peter 3:8-12).

Personal prayer

I now step into you, Father. I step into your truth, into your light, into your presence. I repent for having taken part in any ceremony, ritual, or physical act that opened the door of my soul and spirit to evil. I release all others from every evil word I have ever spoken over them. I repent of all worship or idolatry of other gods. I renounce all vows I made to other gods, and I sever all the power of any bloodletting ceremony and vow. I sever all soul, spirit, and body links and send all ungodly bonds and attachments back to where they came from. Please bring back to me anything from my spirit, soul, and body that the other parties are still holding onto.

I place the precious blood of Jesus Christ between both parties, and in Jesus's name, I bind any powers of darkness that came in through the ungodly connection and command you to leave and to go where Jesus tells you to go. Holy Spirit, please fill those areas where the enemy had control with your love and your presence. Amen

Wait and listen for God's response through your thoughts, feelings, and senses. Write or draw any positive thoughts, mental pictures, feelings, or words God gives you.

NOTES

118

NOTES

16
MY WORSHIP

I was going through a quiet phase with God—not really stagnant, just quiet. Every morning I'd walk out onto my front courtyard, phone in hand, just to bask in the beauty God painted that day. I would start talking to God and go through my basic prayers, but that made me tired. It just didn't seem real, or nearly enough. He seemed a million miles away! But God knows my heart and mind. He knew what I was thinking, and very clearly I heard, Praise me.

I'd always thought praise and worship was for Sunday mornings, so it was a revelation to me that God wanted me to praise him right there in my courtyard. I pulled up some worship music on my phone and hit play. It took a few minutes to feel okay with this.

As each minute passed, I felt more able to sing and just let the songs flow through me. After a few songs had passed, I was jumping up and down, hands in the air, just like at church on Sunday mornings! It was awesome! I felt alive inside again and looked forward to the next morning of praise. Worship became a regular part of my day—as soon as my feet hit the floor, I'd grab a cup of coffee and run outside to hang with God.

There's not enough paper to write down everything this attitude of worship has done to change my life, but I can say it gave me strength to take another step on the path God had for me. I could not see very far; there was only enough light for one step, but that's all it took. The opportunity to worship him is there every morning. Whether or not I choose to worship is up to me, but God always opens that window of time, and choosing to use it is always rewarding.

—Barbara

Worship is one of the most freeing, healing things we can do. We can spend a lot of time examining ourselves and trying to work our way into Jesus, but when we worship we know that we are already in Jesus, and the praise that comes out from that place is like us giving him his breath back. We were created for God's glory and to proclaim his praises. We exist to worship God from the heart.

Our short lives are a gift. They are a moment. A moment in the scheme of a great plan—a great plan of a great God who unconditionally loves us. Let's live our lives loud in worship to him. ~ Kari Jobe

We worship because we are one with our Father, because he is enough, because he is wonderful, because his love knows no bounds, because his sacrifice was astounding, because we are his children, because he comes to give abundant life, and because he is worthy.

There is something sacred about going into a room, shutting the door, and opening up your heart to the King of Kings in song. It's a vulnerable, intimate time of acknowledging his goodness, thanking him for his constant presence, connecting with his heart, and focusing on him. The more focused we become in praise, the more clearly we see and hear his voice, the more our hearts fill up to a bursting point with the fullness of the knowledge of him. And it's not just when we are alone with him—when we join our voices with others, all passionately singing the same words of wonder before him, we storm the heavens with beauty.

> Paul knew hardship. He and the people he journeyed and preached with had many extremely difficult times, including "afflictions, hardships, calamities, beatings, imprisonments, riots, labors, sleepless nights, hunger," but through it all he kept praising God; he knew that in God he had everything he needed (see 2 Cor. 6).

Jesus is enough for your heart. His presence is enough to fill your aloneness, enough to obliterate your darkness, enough to replace your fear, enough to heal your heartache. His hope is enough to displace your hopelessness, his joy is enough to replace your despair, his stability is enough to bring peace to your confusion, his sacrifice is enough to wash away your shame, his power is enough to replace your powerlessness, and his being is enough to validate your own. Your heart is "well" with the Lord. Jesus is enough.

He takes care of your heart, and the matters of your heart are the heart of the matter. The beauty of being in the presence of God when you have no need for expectations to be met is perfect peace. You trust him. And when you fill a room with his praises, either alone or with others, all of heaven wants to join in. You become more aware of his presence, of his healing touch, of his laughter, of his deep, unfathomable love. You are his child in those moments, dancing with reckless joy in the presence of your perfect Father.

And you are also enough.

REFLECTION

Think of your most favorite place in the world to be alone and invite the Trinity (God, Jesus, and the Holy Spirit) to join you. Lean into them, breathe in their presence, and know perfect love—the perfect functional family hug of father, mother (because the Holy Spirit is our guide, comforter, teacher, and counselor), and brother. While you are there, ask him what he wants to give you, what he wants to show you, what he would like to do with your heart. Write or draw his response below.

REFLECTION

Our praise comes from our inner being. Spend some time thanking God for all the things you love about him, and then turn them into a written form of worship. It doesn't have to rhyme and it will never be seen (unless you show it to someone), but this is your personal song of praise to the Father.

TRUTH

What is the truth about worship? Mull over the following Scriptures and write down anything God shows you right now through them.

"Whatever you do, do all to the glory of God" (1 Cor. 10:31).

"I praise you because I am fearfully and wonderfully made; your works are wonderful, I know that full well" (Ps. 139:14).

"But you are a chosen race, a royal priesthood, a holy nation, a people for his own possession, that you may proclaim the excellencies of him who called you out of darkness into his marvelous light" (1 Peter 2:9).

"As servants of God we commend ourselves in every way: by great endurance, in afflictions, hardships, calamities, beatings, imprisonments, riots, labors, sleepless nights, hunger; *by purity, knowledge, patience, kindness, the Holy Spirit, genuine love; by truthful speech, and the power of God; with the weapons of righteousness for the right hand and for the left;* through honor and dishonor, through slander and praise. We are treated as impostors, and yet are true; as unknown, and yet well known; as dying, and behold, we live; as punished, and yet not killed; as sorrowful, *yet always rejoicing;* as poor, yet making many rich; as having nothing, *yet possessing everything*" (2 Cor. 6:4-10; emphasis mine).

As we come to the end of this workbook, we get to look back on the healing God has given you. You've worked together as a team, and you are now even closer to him, fuller in him, and more intimate with him than you were starting out. That's worth celebrating!

Personal Prayer/proclamation

There is a lot of power in a proclamation, so it's fitting to encourage you to speak the affirmations below, aloud and with boldness. They are declarations of the new you—whole, healed, and ready for the next adventure with the Father—and they are a form of worship.

—I am not going to give the devil any glory. It all belongs to God.
—I will live in truth and safety rather than fear and lies.
—I know the power of the truth.
—I am on the path of sanctification—one choice, one truth, one step at a time.
—I choose to live in the truth of the finished work of the cross.
—I will correct or end any relationship in which I am not giving or receiving the freedom to be myself.
—I have rejected all ties to former sins and grievances forever.
—I choose to be whole.
—I choose to destroy lies by living in God's truth and focusing on his beauty. I worship God alone.
—I choose to live in and from the center of God's heart.
—I choose to worship you, God.

Wait and listen for God's response through your thoughts, feelings, and senses. Write or draw any positive thoughts, mental pictures, feelings, or words God gives you.

Follow up: Sometimes God heals in a moment, sometimes he heals over time (because we can only handle a little at a time and he is gentle). There is no formula or time limit to the healing God does in the heart, but this book has given you some tools to help you on your way to wholeness. If you would like more prayer, contact your local church and ask about its inner healing ministry. If it doesn't have one, you may find a local center using the Freedom Resource: thefreedomresource.org/network.html. God bless you!   —Sally

NOTES

126

NOTES

ABOUT THE AUTHOR

Sally Hanan is an Irish import—she moved to Austin, Texas, in 1995 with her husband and young family. As she says, "It was a God thing. You know those few times in your life when you know *that you know* that God wants you to do something? That was one of those two times in my life." (The other time was when she knew she would marry her husband.)

Despite having a nursing degree, Sally stayed at home with her children and homeschooled them, all the while growing in her inner healing and counseling skills by learning from the experts and practicing on trusting friends. Now that her children have grown, she spends her time writing, editing, teaching (at a local school of ministry), counseling, and life coaching.

You can find out more about her by visiting her websites or social media pages:

morethanbreathing.com
facebook.com/morethanbreathing
inksnatcher.com | facebook.com/inksnatcher

If you'd like to contact Sally in order to set up inner healing or life coaching sessions, e-mail her at more@morethanbreathing.com.

OTHER BOOKS BY SALLY

A blind girl has a gift; a father's heart breaks; a young boy in Africa might die; the stepchildren want her dead husband's money.... Read these short snippets of fiction and be prepared to gasp, giggle, and groan. Sally Hanan's insight into the human heart brings depth and richness to her stories, many of them written in a poetic style of prose that flows and gurgles like a country creek.

Joy in a Box is a collection of thirty flash fiction stories, each one the perfect length to go with a morning coffee or a late night cuppa (cup of tea).
Download yours at http://www.smashwords.com/b/1912

ACKNOWLEDGMENTS

First of all, I'd like to thank my pastor, Jeff Newman, for encouraging me to get all of my knowledge and experience onto paper so that our church (the Austin Vineyard) could run inner healing workshops. Without that initial push, I doubt this project would have happened.

Thank you, Bill Vanderbush, for persuading me to become a certified life coach, which is turn made me accountable to my peer coaches (especially Sophia Salazar) to "get 'er done."

Thank you to my Facebook team of supporters who went through my first draft and helped refine the content and pick the cover image. Also a big thank you to those who were willing to share their personal stories—Rose, Kristie, Fran, Ruth O, Yessenia, Miles, Sandie, Dusty, Rita, Barbara, Judith, Ruth L, Britt, Bonnie, Lyn, and Sue.

Thank you, Jan Ackerson of Superior Editing Services, for the superb proofing job. Thank you, Allison Metcalfe of AM Designs—for your many re-dos to get the cover, publishing name, and logo perfect.

And many thanks to all those who gave this project value through their words and actions. I appreciate you all so much!

Made in the USA
Charleston, SC
25 May 2014